Think Again

What are your options?

A Thought-Provoking Book on Awareness and Choice that Everyone is Talking About

By

Matthew Schwam

Thank You

Thank you, God, for this beautiful, challenging, rewarding, and limitless life. Thank you, Jillian, for the truest friendship. Thank you to my children, my greatest teachers. Thank you, Steve, for guiding me home.

Copyright © 2019 by Matthew Schwam

ISBN (Paperback): 978-1-7343326-0-5
ISBN (ePub): 978-1-7343326-1-2

All rights reserved. No part of this publication may be reproduced, distributed, or transmitted in any form or by any means, including photocopying, recording, or other electronic or mechanical methods, without the prior written permission of the publisher, except in the case of brief quotations embodied in critical reviews and certain other noncommercial uses permitted by copyright law. For permission requests, write to the publisher, addressed "Attention: Permissions Coordinator," at the address below.

Although the author and publisher have made every effort to ensure that the information in this book was correct at press time, the author and publisher do not assume and hereby disclaim any liability to any party for any loss, damage, or disruption caused by errors or omissions, whether such errors or omissions result from negligence, accident, or any other cause. This book is not intended as a substitute for the advice of physicians or other mental health professionals.

Matthew Schwam Solutions, Matthew@matthewschwam.com

Ordering Information:
Quantity sales. Special discounts are available on quantity purchases by corporations, associations, and others. For details, contact the publisher at the address above.

Printed in the United States of America

All Rights Reserved

Cover Illustration Copyright © 2019 by Matthew Schwam
Cover design by Matthew Schwam and Vesna Tisma
Book design and production by Slaven Kovacevic
Editing by Danielle Anderson

Contents

Contents v
Foreword. vii

Chapter One – Karma and You. 1
Chapter Two – Freedom in Captivity 7
Chapter Three – Unique Inner Power. 13
Chapter Four – Edging God Out 17
Chapter Five – Here Now. 25
Chapter Six – Truth or False. 43
Chapter Seven – Filters. 47
Chapter Eight – Think About Your Thoughts 51
Chapter Nine – New Statement Technique 55
Chapter Ten – Communicate 71
Chapter Eleven – Remember God. 75
Chapter Twelve – Forgive 79
Chapter Thirteen – Flow 83
Chapter Fourteen – Compassion 89
Chapter Fifteen – Listen. 91
Chapter Sixteen – Just Breathe 95
Chapter Seventeen – Hierarchy of Thought 101

Chapter Eighteen - Appreciate 107
Chapter Nineteen - Self-Identity 111
Chapter Twenty - Ripples 113
THINK AGAIN WORKBOOK. 117
    Unique IP Q&A Worksheet 118
    Fear, Doubt, and Worry Worksheet 119
    Thought List Worksheet 120
    Intention Statements Worksheet 121
    The Future You Worksheet 122
    True or False Worksheet 123
    Unique IP Worksheet 124
    Think About Your Thoughts Worksheet 125
    New Statement Technique Worksheet 126
    Worldview Challenge Worksheet 127
    Worldview Challenge Worksheet 128
    The Giving Worksheet 131
    The Forgiveness Worksheet 132
    Hierarchy of Thought Worksheet 133
    Self-Identity Worksheet 134
    Letter Writing Worksheet 135
    Thoughts and Words Worksheet 136

About the Author. 139

Foreword

Eleanor Roosevelt said, "Remember always that you not only have the right to be an individual, you have an obligation to be one." For the past 200,000 years, human beings have been created by universal intelligence as a complete expression of love, happiness, and limitless potential. You are created already whole and fully equipped with emotions, feelings, and the ability to think, make decisions, change, and grow. As you develop your ability to know the unique gifts delivered within you, you will naturally learn how to manifest your best life with your unique power. You can think of your unique inner gifts as your "Unique Inner Power" or "Unique IP." We all have these unique gifts already built into our DNA; they come naturally. As we gain awareness of Unique IP, we have the potential to be the best in the world in our specific areas of inner power and build our lives upon our built-in foundation for success. As you develop your power, people will be attracted to you and support you with energy and opportunities to advance your life. The more you advance your Unique IP, the more you grow and your alignment with the world deepens.

Unique Inner Power is one of your first great gifts from the universe providing you with a fabulous foundation to live your life as intended. Unique IP comes with the gift of life itself and is yours forever.

> The gift does not perform for you, but rather, it is there to inform you, guide you, and provide you with a platform of ideas and feelings to allow you to grow into your own greatness.

Your "Inner Power thoughts" (or "IP thoughts") are the thoughts that support Unique IP and position you to fully tap into your true powers and be your best self. While the foundation for Unique IP is set for you at birth, the opportunities to strengthen and add to your basis represent the infinite possibilities of your life. Like Unique IP, IP thoughts are inside of you, but IP thoughts represent your thinking about your Unique IP. Since thoughts are largely in your control, the more aware and confident you are in IP thinking, the more you will nurture and advance your Unique IP.

Ego thoughts, on the other hand, are thoughts from the outside world that typically work against your IP thoughts, forcing you to question your own truth. Understanding the ways in which your mind works will protect you from ego-driven, fear-based thoughts that are constantly challenging you. As you think, you speak, and for this reason, you will want to bring Unique IP thoughts to words and actions while cutting ego thoughts at awareness, hence, denying them access to your precious mind space and vocabulary.

Learn to observe yourself as if you were floating weightlessly on a cloud above your physical body, observing feelings, thoughts, words, and actions. When you tell stories about your thoughts, you speak your truth, and when you are aligned with God, you attract powerful, like-minded people to you. As you observe yourself, you learn about how and where your life is aligning. If you recognize your thought process, you might discover that all of your ideas align with love and God but are often conflicted by those that align with outside fear and ego. The better you become at seeing and separating your thoughts, the further you will uncover the distinctions between positive and negative thinking.

Your ego thoughts exist in the world to challenge your IP thoughts. As soon as you start removing and replacing ego thoughts with IP thoughts, you will immediately guide your life to its greatest potential. Fear, doubt, and worry thoughts can be properly used by understanding the lessons and converting to love-based thinking. For example, when you lose a loved one, you can take your feelings of sadness, convert those feelings into a deeper love-based understanding, and eventually use that positive energy to help others who are mourning by showing your compassion and sharing your personal experience. The way forward will be learned when you gain the power of choosing love over fear. For every ego-driven negative thought, there is an equally powerful opposing God-driven thought.

> You get to choose your thoughts. If you make a mistake the first time, you get to think again until you get it right.

Thinking thoughtfully through the moments of your life allow you to author your own book and to be the storyteller of your story. You are the leader of your life. This book is the result of my unwillingness to accept a life of mediocrity and my ability to Think Again.

"Everything can be taken from a man but one thing: the last of the human freedoms— to choose one's attitude in any given set of circumstances, to choose one's own way."

– VIKTOR FRANKL

Chapter One.

Karma and You

HAVE YOU EVER WONDERED ABOUT the things you know intuitively? The things that no one ever taught you, but you know how to do anyway? Ever consider how your personality, worldviews, emotional state, physical condition, mental health, and spirituality have molded you into who you are today?

The answers can be found within your spirit, life experience, learned behavior, and ability to change. In the hierarchy of our beings, the soul is the observer of the body and mind. It is your personal responsibility to listen, understand, and embrace your Unique IP. It is also your personal responsibility to listen to the IP thoughts and ego thoughts that fire away continuously in your mind. Your physical body is largely responding to the results of your spirit-based awareness and mindfulness practices.

Your connection with your soul is equivalent to your connection with your creator. To truly know yourself is to know God.

Why? Because God or another supernatural force is responsible for your life. To achieve this knowing, a deep sense of self-stewardship is required. When you are right with yourself, you are right with the universe and with people in your life, by default.

For our discussion, "God" may be interchanged with whoever/whatever it is that you worship or believe in, whether that be Universal Intelligence, Allah, Christ, Krishna, Buddha, Science, No God, or another source. When you see the word God in this text, feel free to substitute with the source that provides you with the most relevant context. If you don't believe in karma, that's okay too. We are more concerned with developing awareness of your Inner Power as the greatest source of power in your life. This book is about power, self-reliance, value creation, abundance, and happiness, not religion.

The more truthful you are about your inner self, the more you realize self-acceptance. But truth itself will also trigger the need for self-challenge in areas ripe for improvement. You realize that where you are at each moment in time is where you are meant to be. You also realize that you are on this Earth to make a positive contribution to every relationship you touch every day. In order to continuously contribute externally, you need to evolve and improve on the inside.

The more aligned you are with your inner God-given power, the bigger impact you will make in the world. Unique IP guides you to follow, often without tangible evidence of its existence, the spiritual path delivered to you at birth. It is our faith that allows us to find as much comfort in the unexplainable as we do in the tangible. Your Unique IP is like a knowing voice, omnipresent within you, informative, consistent, and forgiving, and it provides all the answers you need to advance your life in a positive direction every day.

Your intellectual capacity to think, when you are aligned with your Unique IP, provides you with a knowing to shower love on everyone and everything in your path. Although an unlikely scenario, if you lived in isolation with no external influence, your only source of knowledge would be expressed with IP thoughts that support your Unique IP. If this were the case, every thought in your life would derive from a deep-rooted connection with God. It would be a pure, uninhibited, unrestricted, unobstructed view of the world, filled exclusively with love and loving thoughts. By recognizing this interesting idea, you can pursue your most ambitious ideas exclusively on your own for as long as you can, before reaching to the outside world for feedback. Typically, you will make mistakes that could have been avoided by engaging sooner with the outside, but almost always you will discover and invent incrementally more by allowing Unique IP to guide the early days of exploration.

The reality is that we are all influenced by outsiders. We are raised by family members or others who have influence over our lives, particularly during our early formidable years. Some of you are fortunate to have received caring and loving support. Others might not have received the same type of positive nurturing. But one thing that all influencers have in common is that they can only teach what they know. Their actions are largely a reflection of their Unique IP and subsequent alignment with God. Their IP thoughts on love and life are in conflict with ego thoughts that have negatively influenced their thinking. Besides our family influencers, we cross paths with thousands of people from the day we are born until the day we pass on. Every person you encounter has the ability to influence your life and you have the ability to influence theirs. Recognizing that we are all impacted by non-aligned influences informs us that others can unintentionally impose negativity on our lives. Just as it is important to filter our own IP thoughts from negative ego thoughts, it is also important to be aware that all individuals face the same challenges maintaining alliances with God and truth. It is your job to be aware of how the people in your life are handling their own internal conversations. This will determine how, if at all, you accept their influence.

> *"When you squeeze an orange, orange juice comes out, because that's what's inside."*
> – Dr. Wayne Dyer

Prior to my father passing away, he and I had been pushed into a family dispute. Caught in a moment of weakness by my elder brother, my father was persuaded to betray me and support a terrible Cain-and-Abel-style idea that aggressively pushed me out of the family business. After my father's death, I resented him for not stepping in and stopping my brother from destroying our family. As I sought advice from my friend and mentor, Steve D'Annunzio, my ego thoughts were telling me that my father knew better and therefore should have done better. In his wisdom, Steve determined that my father did the best he could, with the tools that he had, in the circumstance of his life, and that if I could accept his explanation as my way to think about the situation, I would eventually be able to forgive my father. Fortunately, I was able to replace my ego thought that he could have done better with my IP thought that he did the best he could do. This shift in thinking freed me to love, forgive, and move forward with my life and keep hold of my wonderful memories of my beautiful father.

When you learn to see your true inner self, you will be able to recognize truth in you and in others. *Recognizing how your inner truth relates to another person's inner truth is truth itself.*

The threats to your truth and to your alignment with life are negative influencers that penetrate your purest, most loving thoughts. Every time you encounter a person, directly or indirectly, and a communication occurs—verbally, physically, or otherwise—there is an opportunity to align with love or align with fear, doubt, and worry. The same goes for the choices you make about your inner feelings, even when you are not aware of the outside influencer. It is your job to stay aligned with your inner source of truth so that you only allow into your life the people, thoughts, and experiences that support you. Eventually, unaligned ego thoughts will slip past your filter and turn into words and actions. As you begin thinking ego thoughts, you quickly shift out of alignment. As you begin acting out your ego thoughts and words, your life will begin to move away from you, until you figure it out (awareness) and take action to realign.

"The truth is rarely pure and never simple."
— OSCAR WILDE

When you tend to your mind, body, and spirit each day, you honor yourself and, as a result, the relationships you have with the rest of the world grow. The truest, most loving relationships depend on your ability to love yourself and maintain alignment with God. The relationships in your life will reflect how well you are aligned with your truth. If what you have is pure love, then you are in a beautiful position to give pure love to people who also have the ability to give the same. You can only give what you possess. And karma teaches us that what you give, you also receive.

Chapter Two

Freedom in Captivity

IN LIFE, WE MAY FEEL held captive by things that appear to be out of our control, like environmental conditions, world affairs, corruption, and micro issues like our job, responsibilities, people in our lives and so on. But your spirit is omnipresent and allows you to maintain control of the thoughts and stories you tell yourself about any situation. There is always an ego-driven thought that might leave you feeling helpless, hopeless, and captive. There is also always a positive IP thought that allows you to be empowered over the situation. Actionable thoughts are typically the catalyst to turning the corner from feeling captive to being in charge of your life. It may seem strange to imagine that you can control the thing that appears to be controlling you, but with the right tools and thought process, you can.

    I grew up in a place where bullying, ridicule, and racism was common and unfortunately accepted by many influencers including religious leaders, educators, and moms and dads. During my growing up years, I was the recipient of misaligned negativity. I believe that much of the anger spewed in my direction was due to misunderstanding when my father came out as a gay man after 11 years of marriage and two children, at age 33. I believe that he always knew he was gay, but when he was a teenager, his older brother Jerry was sent for electric shock treatment after coming out. Like many gay men and women did in those days, my dad shut down his truth to avoid the inevitable negative outcome. While the constant anger directed from the community toward my family and me was unpleasant, my awareness of my Unique IP developed quickly from the early age of four years old.

Not only was I watching my father find peace and direction in his life, I was learning a crash-course lesson from him on tolerance, love, and acceptance. I realized that the more I loved and accepted all things that aligned with God, the easier it was to deflect the ignorant words, looks, and ego-driven actions that were flung at me from others.

This is when I discovered my Unique IP. The power I had inside to adapt to major change in my life, see the world from a new perspective, and defend myself and my family's honor made me feel confident and empowered. I didn't realize it then, but I was transforming my initial thoughts of sadness and anger into new thoughts and words of empowerment, compassion, and forgiveness. Before I began to transform my thoughts, I was angry at the people who weren't treating me right. While fighting fire with fire may seem like a good defense, it is a critical mistake that always leads to misalignment with Unique IP. When I was angry, I not only fed the negativity, I also disappointed myself for allowing outside ego thinking into my space. Responding to hate with love was the only way I could align myself with Unique IP and ultimately find peace with myself. It was crazy, but people responded to love and calmed down over time. Eventually, they stopped being so blatant. This does not mean that they stopped their hateful feelings, but I was able to temper their words and actions with mine.

> These thoughts of love freed me to think about solutions and freed the people perpetrating the misaligned actions to slowly shift their own thinking to a better place.

Discovering my Unique IP gave me the ability to extinguish all things negative by focusing my attention on all things positive. A large part of my success has been creating positive thoughts around existing feelings. Feelings are not "bad" or "good," and they are not the driving force behind actions. Whether feelings are filled with hope or riddled with fear, you have a choice about the thoughts and words you select about those feelings. Any feeling on any topic can be turned into a positive thought. Death can be sad and lonely, but it can also create an opportunity to learn how to mourn so that you can comfort others.

Growing up, the simple act of following my Unique IP while returning the fear, doubt, and worry to the senders saved my life. I didn't realize it at the time, but by turning everything positive, I was constantly realigning with myself to remain in love. In the seemingly chaotic situation surrounding me, my inward love was the only place to remain safe. In retrospect, I learned early to focus my attention on the inside when trying to discern right from wrong, good from bad, and truth from opinion. I believed from an early age, out of necessity, that what people thought of me was none of my business. When I bought into outside opinions, I suffered until I was able to realign my internal thinking. It was my opinion of myself that mattered, and with all the negative attention directed my way, I had two choices: either believe the opinions of misguided fear coming at me with all the wrong conclusions for all the wrong reasons, or believe what was coming from the most inner sanctions of my soul. I was encouraged at how resilient I was because I knew from that young age that with God on my side, I would always persevere through the challenges of life. I realized that when something is already part of your essential nature, you don't have to search for it. You just need to lean in and embrace it, even in the face of fear, doubt, and worry.

As I discovered the great heroes in my life, it became apparent that they all had one thing in common. During extremely difficult times surrounding their lives, they went inward, built their Unique IP bonds stronger, and overpowered the outside forces that were imminent threats to their emotional, spiritual, intellectual, and often physical existences.

Viktor Frankl, Wayne Dyer, Anne Frank, and Nelson Mandela are just a few of many people who overcame great odds by doubling down on love in the face of excessive oppression.

Viktor Frankl, the Austrian neurologist and psychiatrist, was a Holocaust survivor. His best-selling book *Man's Search for Meaning* chronicles his experiences as a concentration camp inmate and his ability to find meaning in all forms of existence, which became the focus of his reason to continue living. He attributes his clear and decisive focus on finding meaning for life while surviving against all odds.

Instead of implying the presence of a mental illness related to human experiences such as anxiety, alienation, and depression, his theories of existential psychotherapy saw these experiences as natural stages in the normal process of human development and maturation. He believed that the development of Unique IP involved a focus on an individual's experiences while stressing the individual's freedom and responsibility to facilitate a higher degree of meaning and well-being in his or her life.

Wayne Dyer, the American best-selling self-help author and motivational speaker, spent his first 10 years in a Detroit orphanage after his father walked out on his mother and three small children. Left to fend for himself, Dyer developed a keen sense for his own self-love and connection to God, and he learned early on that self-reliance was required to overcome the adversity surrounding his young life. He spoke deeply about Abraham Maslow's hierarchy of needs theory. Self-actualization was defined as "the desire for self-fulfillment, namely the tendency for the individual to become actualized in what he is potentially." The self-actualized person desires to become more and more what one is, to become everything that one is capable of becoming. Self-actualization would not be possible without absolute alignment with Unique IP and the ability to filter out negativity by focusing exclusively on positive alignment.

Ann Frank, the Dutch-Jewish Holocaust survivor and writer of *The Diary of a Young Girl*, spent two years during

World War II in hiding, where she kept a diary of her most inner thinking. After she and her family were captured and killed, her diary was published. While the world was experiencing chaos, death, and destruction around her, she wrote mostly on her appreciation of God for giving her the ability to express all that was inside.

Nelson Mandela, the revolutionary former president of South Africa, dismantled the practice of apartheid by tackling racism. During his 27 years in prison, Mandela led the revolution and negotiated the end of apartheid and eventually authored a new constitution including land, poverty, and healthcare reforms.

These great heroes of life all faced adversity with a distinctly bonded connection to their Unique IP and an understanding that every feeling of oppression, fear, doubt, or worry could be thought of in the most profoundly positive terms of the user's choosing. Although they lived their lives surrounded by captivity, death, and hatred, their empowered Unique IP freed them to choose how they viewed the world internally.

Chapter Three

Unique Inner Power

"Unique Inner Power," also referred to throughout the book as "Unique IP," is my term for the uniquely coded power delivered to you at birth. It is the foundational tool provided to us by the universe for spiritual, intellectual, and emotional self-awareness and development. It is the powerful energy that makes us whole and allows us to choose love and happiness. When we remain steadfastly aligned with our Unique IP, unwilling to allow negative non-source power to enter our spiritual existence, we thrive through any challenge. First, we need to realize this powerful tool is part of who we are and available unconditionally to us at all times. Our physical, intellectual, emotional, karmic, and spiritual makeup, along with unknown forces, combine to form our Unique IP. Unique IP makes us who we are and creates a pathway to realize our full potential.

In order to realize your Unique IP and live the highest and best life you are capable of, you must be in sync with the universe and with the karmic powers that created you.

Through your Unique IP, your creator has provided you with default opinions and direction for the thoughts, feelings, and decisions you will make over the course of your life. *If you allow your thoughts and words to align with your creator, the actions you take in life will be aligned with the life you are intended to live.*

Unique IP is what makes you uniquely who you are.

You are designed with your own unique code that is unlike anyone else in the world, past, present, or future. While all human beings are very similar, we each have our own unique coding. You have never been duplicated and, as long as the human race remains responsible with its use of advancements in technology, you never will be. Unique IP goes beyond unique genetic coding—it goes beyond DNA and fingerprints. Each of us is also uniquely coded in mind, body, and spirit, fusing infinite combinations that create the one and only you. Within Unique IP, there are the characteristics and traits that make you special and bring love, relationship, value, and support to yourself and others.

Unique IP is maturely advanced in physical, spiritual, and emotional ways that may be a challenge to grasp at first. Faith allows you to contemplate karma as a possibility for how you show up so well equipped with what you need to live a successful, loving, full life. Karma is your soul's delivery of an accumulation of knowing from the unexplainable past. Karma not only delivers your soul to your physical body with a collection of achievements, it also delivers your soul with an assortment of challenges. Your ability to distinguish the achievements from the challenges properly aligns your IP thoughts with Unique

IP. The more you know about what you know, the wiser you become. The more you know about what you don't know, the more astute you become.

Colin Minga was one of my greatest childhood influencers. He was a Baptist, African American man with multiple sclerosis, bound to a wheelchair, teaching health to sixth graders in an openly racist, white suburban, primarily Catholic community. Before I even knew Mr. Minga, I admired him because I related to the racial and social challenges he faced in Nanuet, New York. I'll never forget the first day of class with Mr. Minga. Instead of reviewing his curriculum, which was customary first day activity, he told us about the most important lesson he ever learned from his "mama" when he was our age. He began to recite words, ones I have never forgotten: "He who knows and knows that he knows is wise, listen to him. He who knows and knows not that he knows is a child, guide him. He who knows not and knows that he knows not is ignorant, be compassionate. He who knows not and knows not that he knows not is a student, teach." Mr. Minga's main agenda in the classroom was to drill mama's message into our memories. We recited the words every day, and by the end of the school year, every kid in the class had mama's words etched into their memory. He understood the value of "fake it until you make it." He knew that speaking words created energy, momentum, awareness, and eventually permanent change in thought. For me, the words were one of the greatest gifts of my life. My dear teacher taught me to identify wisdom, vulnerability, compassion, and ignorance.

As you trust and know your Unique IP, so shall you understand your wisdom, vulnerability, compassion, and ignorance. Perhaps this lifetime is your moment to build upon the strengths of your soul and find opportunities to overcome weakness. Your body is nothing more than a vessel for your soul to continue to fulfill its destiny to become the greatest it can be. The soul utilizes your body to implement Unique IP, deepen its understanding and alignment with the universe, and build upon strengths of your past while creating opportunities for the future. If you believe this to be true, then you need not fear the death of your physical body, because your soul will find a new vessel and live infinitely, continuously advancing it's understanding of itself.

The Unique IP Q&A Worksheet in the Think Again Workbook will enable you to answer questions to gain a better understanding of your Unique IP.

Chapter Four

Edging God Out

E GO SUPPORTS FEAR, DOUBT, AND worry. It aggressively fuels the worst parts of us igniting racism, judgement, homophobia, hate, sexism, war, anger, resentment, and the other destructive non-spiritual, low-level ideas of human existence. It is a powerful force that comes at us from all directions, every day. Ego's destructive nature takes us away from our Unique IP out of alignment with God's will. Only the most aware minds can navigate and deflect the ego's desire to penetrate, influence, and interrupt our Unique IP. Ego entices you to question your body image, skin tone, intelligence, kindness, confidence, and vision by introducing you to conflicting external points of view. If you allow ego-themed thoughts to override your IP thoughts, you will forget that you were born perfect. You will begin to allow ego thoughts to break you down, create insecurity, speak words of self-doubt and fear, and potentially align yourself with people who have also fallen into this same trap. Upon connecting with people thinking ego thoughts, you need to be aware enough to wake up, get out, and return to Unique IP. The longer you stay centered on ego, the deeper the problems will get and the further away from true Inner Power you will go.

Ego penetrates into the intangible world of spirituality. It listens exclusively to the outside world and, like a hawk focused on killing its prey, finds you in moments of weakness and attacks. The ego, in some circles, is an acronym for "Edging God Out." It provides you with the opposing viewpoint to the God-given perspective delivered and designed specifically to align you with your highest and best self. Unique IP is a spiritual foundation for positive thinking upon which to build your life. Ego, on the other hand, is absorbed and learned after arrival; it is born from the perspective of the influencers who interact with you and your external environment at large. Ego is designed to break down your Unique IP foundation and concurrently test your will, requiring great strength to protect your inner integrity and self-worth.

Inner Power thoughts are your purest, most honest, unfiltered thoughts that trigger your words and actions in the true story of your life. They inform you in the simplest ways on self-love, forgiveness, tolerance, kindness, equality, spirituality, communication, family, and friendship.

Ego thoughts, on the other hand, are thoughts provided from the outside world. When used properly, ego thoughts can be utilized for your context and contemplation, but never for your blind acceptance. They are there to help you develop awareness so that you can choose properly and see your Inner Power in crystalized perspective. *It is only your lack of awareness that confuses you when you are unable to clearly distinguish between your Inner Power and ego thoughts.* By listening from the inside, you have a daily opportunity to stop, look, and listen to your story.

You tell the story of your perception of life every time you communicate. And you alone are choosing, with your words, how to articulate the story. When you tell it, people around you support whatever you say because they subconsciously trust that you have filtered your thoughts properly. *The people in your life are a direct reflection of the thoughts that you create about your life and the words and actions that follow those thoughts. In other words, the people you create in your story show up in your life instantly.* When you are in learning mode, teachers appear. When in teaching mode, students appear. When in Unique IP mode, Unique IP people appear. And when in non-source power mode, non-source people appear.

Truth and reality are created every moment. The people in your path sense the energy you are emitting and only those who possess parallel energy will be attracted to you at that moment. We call these attractor patterns. Typically, attractor patterns are positive or negative. Like attracts like.

If you are attracting attention that is out of sync with the person you know you are destined to be, then you need to examine the story you are telling and the subsequent energy you are emitting. The more you tell it, the more support that lines up in your life to make it come true. If the story is unfiltered, you might be attracting unwanted people, ideas, experiences, and things in your life that do not belong to you. These items tend to come in the form of distractions, turmoil, negative attractors, and all the things that you did not intend to manifest but did because of your own state of unawareness.

Your energy is an intangible force that sends ripples—positive, negative, or neutral—wherever you go. We are interconnected with all people and things, creating a universal relationship of dynamic exchange with the world. Pay attention to your state of energy; it affects everyone. People feel everything about your presence in this world, including your openness, love, and connectedness, but also your fear, doubt, worry, and insecurities.

Support your greatest energy with words that resonate with the people you want in your life.

Deliver strong, powerful energy and watch it move through their bodies; know that the ripple will impact the next person they meet. When we are centered in Unique IP, our love, happiness, honesty, and truth ripple everywhere. When we are negative, we create spiritual inconsistencies that throw our minds and bodies out of balance, which in turn, throw our relationships out of sync.

An unaware mind is one that is out of sync with God and our own quest to identify and manifest destiny.

Be cautious to avoid inadvertently passing your fears onto your children by talking about them out loud. Your children will imitate you, as children do, and develop unfiltered stories that become part of their vocabulary and immediately part of their inherited reality. Every time they tell the story, people believe them and take action on the information accordingly. They can easily develop a weak thought, which in turn attracts weak people who hear, understand, and like to participate in conversations about things that they are afraid of.

While you might be speaking honestly about a fear that you are working on, your children more easily adapt false ideas of fear than an aware-minded adult. They can easily become fearful of things if supported and reinforced by their influencers. Somehow, fear can become acceptable and even comfortable. As human beings, we tend to gravitate toward the familiar, even if the familiar is not beneficial. Your spoken thought could just as well have been about something positive like fearlessness or ambition, but in this example, it is fear. As you constantly work to align with your own Unique IP, you have the power to decide to express your most powerful thoughts to your children.

> "Love is the great miracle cure. Loving ourselves works miracles in our lives."
> – Louise Hay

Have you ever noticed that, culturally, we see much more bad news than we see good? Television, newspapers, magazines, and evening news believe that the stories of human problems earn better ratings than stories of human victories. The media understands that your ego thrives on fear, doubt, and worry. Their goal is to get you to tune in externally and lose sight of your internal compass. Their mission is to sell advertising and make money. Media understands the power of subconscious thinking driven by ego. You will need to decide if the media information you are asking for and receiving is in sync with your Unique IP. I decided a long time ago that most of the information from these sources weakens me and I largely stopped allowing it access to my precious mind space. What the news does not understand is that if they would have the courage to report on all the goodness in the world, they would play a big role in assisting human beings to trust and use their Unique IP. Humans would more naturally gravitate to good news and solution-oriented stories as a result.

> "The only thing that can save the world is the reclaiming of the awareness of the world. Whoever controls the media and the images, controls the culture."
> – ALLEN GINSBERG

Meditation is an exercise that encourages your mind to observe your thoughts, to be still, to stop the inner chatter, and to walk away with a cleaner thought pallet. The clean pallet allows you to step away from a few thoughts, for a few minutes and quietly evaluate what's happening in your inner thought world. Daily morning meditation is a way to set a clear intention to align with spirit. By aligning with spirit, you force unaligned ego thoughts out of your mind. Truth always enforces power over falsehood. When you meditate, you empower your mind to observe Unique IP and ego thoughts from a quiet, contemplative, and neutral position. This places you in a powerful position to be introspective before the phone rings, text messages ding, and emails flow in. When the day gets going, your goal is to think about it in the most positive, aligned way possible with as little ego interference as you can. The morning is the awakening of the day. For this reason, it is the most fitting time to awaken our awareness and to realign with our Unique IP.

The Fear, Doubt and Worry Worksheet in the Think Again Workbook will enable you to write down the feelings that trigger your fear, doubt, and worry and the results you receive when you engage.

Chapter Five

Here Now

The moment we are guaranteed in life is the one that we are in right now. Now is the most relevant time for you to be the biggest and best version of yourself. No matter what you are doing minute by minute, that will be your time to be fully present and engaged with your growth and greatness.

If you are wasting this moment reliving troubles of the past in your thoughts, then you are missing the only moment of opportunity you have to fully engage in your best possible life. If you think thoughts of regret, self-doubt, and guilt over the past, then you are effectively reliving the emotional experience and compounding the impact by not being here now. When you take an experience from the past and pull it to the present, you recreate the very action that you are contemplating in regret, self-doubt, and guilt. Instead of experiencing it only once, you experience those negative thoughts and feelings twice. The act of thinking weak thoughts weakens you and triggers your ego to step up, edge God out, and misinform your Unique IP in hopes of holding you hostage in fear, doubt, and worry.

> If you are wasting time thinking of the past or future, the *opportunity cost of that time is what you would have otherwise been thinking of and taking action on to impact today.*

Now is the only time you have to change your life; the past is gone and cannot be changed. Reliving it brings no positive gain and only sets you back. Instead, focus on listening to your inner voice guiding you exclusively toward positive thoughts that align with your Unique IP.

The voice of your ego's future is dumping fear, doubt, and worry into your unfiltered thoughts based on pessimistic views of potential events. On the other hand, the voice of your Unique IP's future is providing goals and dreams that align with what you are doing right now to create the biggest and best life for yourself. Both voices show up every day. Your ability to manifest your Inner Power thoughts is entirely dependent on your awareness to recognize the difference between outside ego thoughts and Unique IP thoughts. The thoughts, words, and actions you choose right now and the feelings they influence affect your progress and ability to align with Unique IP.

The Thought List Worksheet in the Think Again Workbook will enable you to directly compare your outside ego thoughts with your inner Unique IP thoughts.

> *"Fear may come true from that which one is afraid of."*
> — VIKTOR FRANKL

To fully harness your dreams, begin by knowing your Unique IP and seeing those dreams clearly. Manifesting future dreams involve taking snapshots in your mind's eye of what your life looks like in the future as your best self in your best life. If you are a visual person, you can create a vision board. You might prefer to write a list that represents the future. Whatever your method to see things clearly, presenting your future vision in a defined way positions you to take your next step to achieving your goals. Stay focused on what you can do now to move forward toward the vision.

We should always have a future vision of the better version of ourselves. But *this vision is not to negate the person you are today in the present moment.* The present moment you, be assured, is in perfect harmony with the universe. You are strong, courageous, fully able, and perfect as you are right now. You are exactly where you are supposed to be. Knowing this allows you to accept the past, see the future, and create balance in the present. Knowing that you are perfect as you are also provides confidence to take steps each day to be better than you were the day before. One step at a time is all you need. Life is not a sprint. Self-actualization does not happen overnight. We are all too aware of the obstacles that we face. Each day, stay focused on one small improvement that makes you better today than you were the day before.

> "I didn't come this far to only come this far."
> – UNKNOWN

Ego-driven excuses stop your progress. Your constant quest to be your best should never end.

You may be perfectly content with your life and that's okay. But if you stop and think about it, you have an infinite number of things on your list to improve.

Human beings are designed with capacity for constant emotional, physical, and spiritual growth. *If your creator delivered you to another day of life on Earth, you have a karmic obligation to act upon your Unique IP, which ultimately makes the world a better place.*

Don't be content with being the 80 percent version of yourself. Your ability to continuously recognize your unending capacity to contribute to the world is a central byproduct of your awareness of Unique IP. The more you know yourself, the more you know, the more you grow, and the happier you will be.

> *"The future depends on what we do in the present."*
> – MAHATMA GANDHI

Imagine a life where you were always adding value, always there, always grateful, always with yourself, and always fully present. That life is possible when you remain connected to your Unique IP and remain aware of your thoughts in the present moment. Do you know how much time you spend absent from what's happening in your own life while you think about things that have already happened or future things that might or might not happen? Awareness of your thoughts will trigger presence of mind to every moment.

Have you ever imagined something happening in the future and then made impactful, fear-based decisions on the possibility of that something actually happening? Did you change important thoughts or actions based on something you made up in your mind, later to realize that the thing you feared—the reason you changed your path—never happened?

If you are a business owner and you lose an important account, you might labor over what you could have done in the past to keep the account. All the while, you might also contemplate the future and begin to worry about not replacing the customer and maybe even going out of business as a result. As soon as you visualize yourself going out of business, you subconsciously begin to understand the steps that happen between today and when that event takes place. If those steps begin to manifest, you might somehow be comfortable, particularly since you have already thought about it, providing counterproductive familiarity. Now continue the imaginary story and project how the outcome would have been different had you created a new statement with IP thoughts as opposed to the ego thoughts that created the turmoil. Can you see that you made the choice? Can you see how easy it would have been to shift the outcome? It was in your control the whole time. And it still is in your control.

You can absolutely recreate and retell any story in your life that has you out of sync with your purpose. Tell the new story, believe it, discuss it, trust it, live it. You will attract supporters instantly and you will be on your way to your new reality.

When you think of making changes in your life that will create a big impact, it can feel overwhelming. We feel like we need to make monumental efforts to get monumental results. While we do have to make big efforts and commit to hard work upfront to achieve the desired results, the effort-to-reward ratio is disproportionate. Concentrated effort upfront creates immediate impact and long-term positive change. The immediate changes are proportionate to the initial effort, but the long-term change is disproportionately beneficial. *In other words, when you implement change and create new patterns in your life to make the new story sustainable, the compounding effects that show up in your life are your lifelong miracles.*

Think of a sea vessel that leaves North America on a journey to Europe. If that vessel is off by one degree, the vessel could land in Africa. The point is, just a one-degree shift will produce dramatic results. Since ego thoughts and IP thoughts are in perpetual conflict, the shifts go both ways. Our goal is to create mostly positive, one-degree shifts, one at a time. The space between your decision to shift and the result of that shift is your journey.

For 20 years, I ran two successful companies. While I was learning to live in alignment with the creative parts of my Unique IP, I struggled to be present in my personal relationships. My vision for my family was and remains loving, cohesive, and bonded, but my present moment thoughts, for most of my years in business, were consumed with the challenges of the day. My inability to be present squashed progress on my vision for the incredible family experience that I envisioned. As a result, my relationships with my wife and children were not developing as I had desired. Instead of delivering a consistent flow of love and support, I was in constant conflict with my Unique IP and misaligned thoughts entering my space, unfiltered, from the challenging external environment that commanded my attention. Misaligned thoughts, over time, put me squarely out of sync with my Unique IP. Unique IP represents all of oneself and cannot be compartmentalized. I have always known that who you are anywhere is who you are everywhere. It took me a long time to model my career in a way that frees me to be equally as impactful in my personal life as I am in my business life. When I stopped clinging onto unhealthy relationships with my companies, I freed myself to nurture love and happiness by holding my wife and children.

> "A man is but the product of his thoughts;
> what he thinks, he becomes."
> – MAHATMA GANDHI

You are usually fearing, doubting, and worrying about something that you think might happen in the future based on information that you possess today. Whenever you find yourself worrying about a future event that may or may not happen, you can either choose a thought that contemplates the negative or choose a positive thought to create a solution now. When you focus on the solution, you are doing something in the present moment to change the reality of the future. Your alternative is to support the fear.

> "Live this day as if it were your last. The past is
> over and gone. The future is not guaranteed."
> – DR. WAYNE DYER

If someone did you wrong and you are thinking about it now, remember that they did the best they could with what they had to work with. Resentments and anger in your thoughts and conversation will recreate resentments and anger in your present moments. What you think about the person of your thoughts might not impact that person at all. You and the people in your present moment are the only ones impacted by the perceived problem from the past. Instead of talking about the problem, discuss the lesson learned, how you could have done better, what you intend to do the next time something similar comes up, and how you forgive the people involved. Don't rehash the problem, just rethink how you can make an improvement.

"Be here now" are the words often echoed by the late great Dr. Wayne Dyer. He cleverly switches the letters of "here now" around to spell "nowhere," just to emphasize how close we are to being present when we are sleepwalking and how vulnerable we are to losing sight of the present and slipping into another reality. This is why self-awareness is so important.

> The present moment is the most meaningful moment that you have in your life.

The last moment is in your past and is now just a memory. If you use the last moment for context, you will relate that moment to the present moment and take actions accordingly. If you use that moment as a predictor, you might prejudice and repeat what you've done, due to your preconceived notions of action and reaction that you bring to the present. If you are changing every day to become a bigger, better version of yourself, then your life is a continuous progression; repeating the past will only stall that progression forward. Your ability to make change is the most important part of your life's progression. Decisions are made daily on what parts of the past to bring forward and what parts of the past to leave behind.

Just because a person, place, thing, or thought was in your life yesterday, does not mean it has to remain in your life today. When you use today as your compass, you can ask if parts of your past still belong in your life. If the answer is no, then you need to ask how and when to leave it behind. If the person, place, thing, or thought continues to enhance your life, feed your Unique IP, and provide happiness, then it gets to stay and move forward with you. If you are aware that you are making these choices, then you will bring forward only parts of your life that add value. *Upon further examination, you will find that the parts you leave behind likely filtrated from the outside and the parts you bring forward were there all along.*

Our visions are based on how we see ourselves in the future, making the future vision very important. But what we do about it right now is what matters most of all. Now is the only moment that you can impact and it's the only moment that is guaranteed. It makes you wonder how anyone could possibly complain right now, given the fact that it may be the last thought and communication they ever have.

The challenges that show up in your life are not what should interest or concern you. Instead, how you manage your feelings with powerful thinking through those circumstances and ultimately the lessons you take away are what matter. The lessons and positive adjustments to your Unique IP will provide you with fuel to advance.

The past can be seen as a series of reference points. The references are not indicative of who you are, but rather of where you used to be. Your ability to become the very person that God put you on this Earth to be is the power you possess that outweighs any mistake that was previously made.

If you allow the challenges of your past to define you, then you negate your ability to make progress now and in the future. It is unfair to permanently punish yourself or others for mistakes that were made, especially if those mistakes have been acknowledged and change is desired. Lessons from the past are valuable to pull forward, but defining labels need to be removed and left behind. If you start every day with a fearless freedom to go wherever your inner spirit moves you, then you will grow and develop all the fibers of your being.

> "I wish I could show you when you are lonely or in darkness the astonishing light of your own being."
>
> – HAFIZ

Instead of shining a spotlight on your fully manifested future, focus on the next step that you can take today to move you closer to the future you. It's the implementation of process that happens now which brings you closer and closer to your vision, closer to God, to yourself, and to the people in your life, one day at a time. If you become tangled up today in the future outcome of your vision, you might be discouraged by the gap between today's reality and the vision.

Imagine if your task was to swim 300 yards across a lake and you set an unachievable time to finish. The only way to make the swim is to go one stroke at a time, at a pace that your body can confidently manage. Rather than think about the finish line, you need to think about each stroke. Make each stroke as technically accurate and as good as it can be. Don't worry about the last stroke or the next one. Just focus on the stroke you are now taking. Follow the process and you will make progress, eventually realizing your vision of crossing the finish line. This analogy can be universally applied to sports, business, relationships, and most other parts of your life.

Focus on being present and accepting your current experience. Focus on your emotions and how they feel in your body.

Choose to be in the presence of love and let life guide your words and actions. The choice will transform relationships, starting with yourself.

Find beauty in what is, not what you are hoping for. Life is a process. Processes are developed so that we can organize our growth with realistic expectations. Each step of the process is required and happens in the present moment.

Nothing happens until something moves. Awareness needs to be the trigger for new thought, which then triggers words and eventually action. Action leads us to new realities. Even if you don't have all the answers at this moment, if you have the thoughts and words in place, you are positioned to take action.

> *"The day came when the risk to remain in the bud was more painful than the risk it took to blossom."*
> — Anais Nin

Many people require research and analysis prior to taking action. Others are quicker to move forward and listen mostly to their gut instincts, often moving impulsively into areas that they know little or nothing about. A balance of caution and instinct will serve you well when contemplating meaningful life change. If a pattern of problems persists in your life, you know that repeating the actions consistently replicates the same problems. Making the first decision to remove the action that triggers the problem should be easy and require little research. The questions to ask are these:

1. What problem needs to be solved?
2. What action needs to be replaced?
3. What is the best possible outcome?
4. What action can you take to replace the old action?

The right answers and best practices may not be available until you start the journey. It is worth noting that your journey started the day you were born and is ever changing and evolving, so this moment of creating intentional change, again, is perfectly healthy.

There is never a good time to stop growing and never a bad day to make a good decision. Even if you have met challenges and made bad decisions in the past, it's time to move on. With each step forward, new ideas develop and guide you to realize your aligned vision. This is a process. We progress one step at a time. Talking about being a bigger, better version of yourself is a good first step. Acting like the new version of you before it's true and realized is integral to becoming the new version. "Fake it 'til you make it" suggests that the day you align your thoughts with your Unique IP and decide to proceed, you need to give yourself permission to think of yourself as if you were already the fully realized person you are seeking to become. The more you think, act, and feel like the fully realized version of yourself, the faster the new way will become the new reality.

As you reach new levels of awareness, creation of new consistent patterns of thought and behavior will come naturally. Your belief in God and in the power that was given to you is all you need to manifest and manage your growth.

Your ability to make good decisions on areas ripe for improvement and replacement is critical to starting each phase of growth. *Implementation requires tools of awareness, a process, discipline, spiritual habits, experience, experimentation, and time to develop, practice, and get it right.* While you are getting it right, you will be expected to make your share of mistakes. Even if your direction is in alignment with your Unique IP, mistakes are inevitable, required for your learning, and should never shake your trust in the journey. Mistakes are just lessons in disguise and invitations to improve.

You have often heard your Unique IP clearly tell you what you are supposed to do or who you are meant to be. But if the who and what are not accompanied by the how, you might not know what to do about the thought and you may pass it over in favor of repeating something that you already know. Usually, the thing that you already know is ready to be replaced with the new thing that you don't fully have a handle on yet. If you have the awareness of a new replacement thought and the courage to accept it as possible, you will accept it as your new reality upon implementation. Accepting your thought as your reality is the first step toward manifesting and making it happen.

The Intention Statements Worksheet in the Think Again Workbook will enable you to state your intentional ideas and write how the ideas will change your life.

I was born with Unique IP to create physical beauty in the world from my imagination. For a long time, I lacked the awareness and confidence to manifest my spiritual destiny to create and I allowed myself to be labeled as a salesman. There is nothing wrong with that label, but my true label was meant to be creator. In fact, I felt limited by the labels and realized that labels in our lives were there to identify our function in a particular situation, create discipline, and build order in a multidisciplinary setting. But labels also have a tendency to box people in and to limit expansion and growth. Since people around us tend to believe what we tell them about ourselves, it is easy to see how a label would make it very easy for everyone to stop wondering what your function is. Imagination is tied directly to wonderment, and if we stop imagining about our unlimited potential and start narrowly defining ourselves, the energy for growth will fizzle.

As soon as I took my leap of faith to trust my inner creative gift, I began to find the tools needed within me to become great at my craft. I was being held back by false beliefs that wouldn't allow me to fully and properly express myself. As soon as I changed my mind and lifted the label, I changed the story that I was telling the world. While I still have descriptions, they are more than words and as broad as I can make them: creator, entrepreneur, writer, advocate, father, husband, son, friend.

> *It takes courage to declare your intention to do something you have never done before. Don't allow fear, doubt, and worry to hold you down or steer you back to old patterns.*

Ultimately, your old patterns might be well suited for you, but you are cheating yourself if you don't listen to the voice inside yearning to redefine those patterns and discover your full potential.

> *"I'd rather take a step and fail than spend all my life wondering what it could have been."*
> — JOEL OSTEEN

Your thoughts are life's way of calling you to advance your very self. Life constantly challenges you to take a chance on yourself. You just need to believe that you would not have the thought if you didn't have that ability within you to manifest and implement. Just because you've never done it before does not mean you cannot do it now. Just because something has been done differently in the past doesn't mean that there's not a better way now. If you had the thought, then it must be possible. Challenging the norm should be the norm.

> *"If you want to recreate the world, look at it with fresh eyes. Today, have the intention to see one thing with fresh eyes, as if for the first time. Look without memory of the past. Sometimes the hardest thing to see is the thing we've been looking at the longest."*
> — Deepak Chopra

"Fools rush in" does not mean that you shouldn't take action on your thought with an immediate decision to pursue. To the contrary, it suggests that you follow your heart decisively now, but allow your decision to unfold and manifest over time naturally. Do not force the decision into action before it is ready. With every great vision comes a great thought process, which in turn is the story that triggers the manifestation of the vision. The story represents the process, the how to. It may start as a simple outline with key milestones, with not a single detail on how to reach your vision, and this is okay. *If you are operating in Unique IP, you will trust that while the process requires planning, it also requires faith and needs to unfold as you experience life through your new lens.* Some mistakes have to be made and lessons have to be learned along the journey to the final vision.

You will likely find that the initial path of your journey might not be exactly right to fully realize your vision. Your ability to adapt and make intelligent modifications along the way will serve you well and keep you on track. You should not mistake determination with rigidity. Determination will allow your inner compass to trust the audibles that need to be called along the way to get you aligned with your Unique IP vision. Without the first decision to create change and without a decision-making process that you trust, you might have never started the process. Or worse, you might have started on an ego-driven journey influenced by forces outside of your Unique IP.

The Future You Worksheet in the Think Again Workbook will enable you to identify and compare the Current You with the Future You and take action today.

> *"Do not go where the path may lead, go instead where there is no path and leave a trail."*
> – Ralph Waldo Emerson

The journey is often more valuable and enriching than the final destination. Your willingness and ability to constantly recheck and adjust is pivotal to your growth.

> *"The secret to getting ahead is getting started."*
> – Mark Twain

Chapter Six

Truth or False

LIFE IS A PROCESS THAT requires intentional thought and faith to trigger action. Intentional thought and faith develop from practice and experience. The more you trust your inner self, the more you will find your most balanced and aligned self. The more you succeed, the more you will trust the process. Success never comes from following your ego's fear-based reactions to the external environment.

Here's an exercise to test the idea. Think of an action that you took that triggers feelings of regret. Now think of yourself in the future repeating that same action and worrying about the consequences that repeating the mistake will create. Finally, right now, tell yourself as clearly as you can who you need to be and what you have to do to change the old action once and for all, so that you never have to confront the negative consequences of the old action again. You will be amazed at how this process creates a new reality around this subject matter that filters through Unique IP and aligns with the best of who you really want and deserve to be, or with the result that you really want and deserve to have.

When you don't have the proper tools to correct an unreliable thought or action, you use excuses instead. *Excuses are used to justify actions in your life that are clearly out of alignment.* Excuses include phrases such as, "That's just the way I am," "That's how I was raised," "I have a temper because...," "I have guilt because I am...," "I hide my emotions when...," etc. The list goes on and on. You have dozens of them that you might be thinking about and acting upon every day.

When factual evidence exists to prove that an action has occurred, then the fact that the action occurred is true. If you or someone else sees or hears with their eyes and ears, you have evidence for truth. Feelings and emotions that occur after a true event are largely out of your control; they just appear in your space and force you to deal with them. The opinions and interpretations about the feelings you have are not based in fact. They are merely your subjective thoughts. While it may be true that you decided to like or dislike an experience in your life, the fact that it happened and that it left you with emotional feelings are the only truths.

What's more powerful is that most of us think that the feeling is largely beyond our control; it is just how we feel and therefore it is true. But since feelings are actually a byproduct of your worldview, how you feel about a fact is largely influenced by how you feel about life.

The facts are the only truth. The rest of it—including your feelings—is a product of your thinking that you have chosen.

> The unintended consequence of confusing truth with opinion is subconsciously turning opinion into truth by attaching it to the facts.

This will create problems in your life if you are not aware of your thinking mind. You might have a dear friend who was uncharacteristically rude to you on separate occasions within the span of a couple weeks. After unsatisfactorily gaining an understanding of why this was happening, you might conclude that your friend has changed and is no longer a good person. As a result, you might distance yourself or even end the friendship. However, one day, you might ask yourself if it was true that your friend changed, only to find out that your friend had been dealing with serious health issues and hadn't come to terms with the threat this was causing. In fact, the behavior had nothing to do with the friend's character, but rather everything to do with the circumstance they were facing in that moment. So often, we place judgement on another's character when understanding and context are most required to understand what's happening. Learning the truth is always the best way to understand and avoid taking actions on our false beliefs.

The Indian proverb "what you think about me is not of my business" provides insight to preventing challenges that occur when opinions are received as truth. Opinions are nothing more than the thoughts and subsequent words discussed about something that actually happened.

When something is clarified as true, it may trigger a feeling that may not be in your control at that moment.

But how you think about your feeling certainly is. You may hear about a conflict, feel bad, and subsequently think, "This is terrible." Alternatively, you may feel bad and choose to think, "Something good will come from this."

The True or False Worksheet in the Think Again Workbook will enable you to evaluate the beliefs you have about yourself, others, and the world around you. If you find your statements to be false, time to think again.

Chapter Seven

Filters

YOU ARE NOT EXPECTED TO blindly trust and regurgitate what you see and hear. Think of an internal filter inside your mind that all information has to pass through before you will allow the information to penetrate and reflect who you are. If you take information in from the outside world and fail to run it through your filter, you are simply repeating someone else's thoughts and potentially responding to ego's opposing and harmful information. The influences you accept from the outside world must be in alignment with the personal requirements of your inner world. If outside influence enters you unfiltered, you will sleepwalk into a story that no longer belongs to you. You will become a character in someone else's story. *When you are no longer the writer of your story, your life is at the mercy of the new author.*

If ego thoughts bypass the filter, they will take you out of alignment and cannot be trusted. Alternatively, if love-driven thoughts filter through to your words, they will align you with God and the universe to exponentially enhance your life.

Having faith in people is good, but having blind faith is not okay. *People in your life can be trusted but must be verified through the guiding principles of your heart.* The personal threat to your Unique IP is unfiltered and unverified energy absorption. If you think of your Inner Power as that part of you that you value most, you will understandably want to protect it. If you believe that you are your thoughts and that your life follows your thoughts, then protecting your mind is high priority.

Inner Power filtration happens when we filter thoughts through awareness. Inner Power filtration will allow you to choose whether your thoughts are in alignment with the guiding principles of your Unique IP. Ego will immediately challenge your Unique IP with an opposing view and with one purpose: to make you right, with no regard for spiritual truth or alignment. It is enough for the ego to know that you thought the ego thought and, therefore, it must be right. To convince you, it will find ways to support you and force you to be right. Ego can make choices around filtering and alignment confusing.

> *"Happiness is when what you think, what you say, and what you do are in harmony."*
> – MAHATMA GANDHI

All human beings share a basic need to be happy. As previously noted, the ego would rather be right than be happy. To the contrary, Unique IP thoughts are delivered by universal love and naturally reside in you to guide you to happiness. If we think of Inner Power thoughts as providing a powerful filter, we can think of ego thoughts as providing a forceful result. An IP thought will move seamlessly, yet assertively through a powerful filter and align with your Unique IP. Ego thoughts meet with cosmic resistance while attempting to force their way into your Inner Power. Awareness of power and force is an important tool for growth.

When you recognize that your ego is involved to create or validate your misaligned thinking, you will seek to discover what is required to validate truth. Being right and truth prevailing are not always in alignment. As you seek to uncover the truth, you will naturally remove and replace ego thoughts.

It is your spiritual knowing that allows you to overcome your ego-thinking mind. Your spiritual knowing is more simply understood as your intuition or self-alignment. One might also think of intuition as subconscious knowing. It's when you know, but you don't know how you know. Notwithstanding, you will require intentional thinking to recognize and listen to the power of your spirit.

> It is your spiritual responsibility to recognize your ego and remove it from your life by surrendering it to God.

God thoughts, unlike ego thoughts, seek truth, balance, wisdom, humility, and growth. God is not attached to making you right or wrong. God wants you to find your way to perfect harmony with your unique truth and happiness, to be true to no one but yourself, with no influencers other than God. Surrendering misaligned thoughts to God sets conditions for the removal and replacement of those thoughts.

One great filter for answering ego thoughts that challenge Unique IP is to ask yourself, "If God were in the room, what would God have me say now?" *If you answer life's questions from this unique perspective, you will find the pure, untouched words that flow through you as if you are a vessel for truth.* People with spiritual knowing and awareness are in control of their thoughts, aware of their gifts, and able to decisively distinguish between love's power and fear's force with ease and confidence.

The last piece is absolute trust in yourself as a thinking, spiritual human being to implement thoughts and actions required to fully realize your Unique IP.

Inner Power is based on the principle that everything you need in life at any given moment is already within you.

Your mission is to be one with your Unique IP, and hence, one with the universal source of creation. It is when you look inside with pure and authentic intentions without outside influence that you find the lessons that God delivered. If your awareness allows, Unique IP will be the source of all things powerful and positive in your life.

Unique IP Worksheet in the Think Again Workbook will enable you to identify your Unique IP and your thoughts about how special you are.

Chapter Eight

Think About Your Thoughts

INNER POWER IS FORGIVING. IF your power to love leads you to unintentionally hurt someone, you will also have the power of love to heal the hurt. When you re-filter and realign yourself with your Unique IP, you can create new meaning to a subject, forge thoughts around it, forgive yourself, and move forward toward manifesting new and improved love.

The key to maintaining Unique IP is consistently feeling, listening, challenging, aligning, realigning, and believing in yourself. As soon as you identify the powers within you that make you the best in the world at what you are doing, who you are, and how you are behaving, then you will adjust your ways of being to consistently filter through those powers.

Do you see what I am saying? If you can see what you are saying, you can decide on a process and begin taking steps to realize the vision that you see. Since your words follow your thoughts, what you are thinking and saying is extremely relevant. Therefore, thinking about your thoughts is something that you should constantly be doing. If you do not observe yourself, build on strengths, course correct weaknesses, and deflect ego, who will?

Thinking about your thoughts requires you to create imaginary space between you the thinker and you the observer of you the thinker.

Imagine your spirit-self floating above your human-self with God-like insight to your human-self's every thought. Allow your spirit-self to make observations about your human-self's thoughts. You will position yourself to see yourself exposed and manage accordingly from there.

The following is an excerpt from six recent days in my life that I documented in an effort to create awareness for myself by thinking about my thoughts.

After several days of waiting, I received a phone call from Dr. K, my orthopedic surgeon, stating that the radiologist discovered an "incidental finding," in my MRI for a shoulder injury. A large mass was lodged in the back side of my right shoulder. . A second MRI was ordered to further investigate the mass. My first feeling was fearful, but I was able to see the fear and reassure myself instead that everything would be great.

After 6 long days waiting for the results of the second MRI, Dr. K called during dinner and said "I spoke with the radiologist and he believes this mass inside your shoulder is a malignant sarcoma." This was not the news I created in my thoughts and my eyes welled up, but luckily, the tears did not have a chance to roll down my face for the kids to see before I excused myself from the dinner table and went up the steps to the privacy of my bedroom. My wife Jillian followed right behind me and we sat together with one ear each pressed against the phone. As we listened, he began to use words like "muscular sarcoma," "soft tissue," "surgery," "needle biopsy," "radiation," and "chemotherapy." We looked at each other in disbelief.

I made a decision while I was listening that he might be wrong. By creating this possibility, it meant to me that the radiologist's opinion was not necessarily true. He told me to make an appointment with Dr. T, the hospital's specialist in muscular sarcoma's. I knew deep down that worrying about this would not help me or Jill and faught off my fear, hugged my wife, said I love you, heard her say I love you, told her we got this and heard her say we always do. And we went back to the dinner table.

I naturally, but mistakedly spent some of the night researching online, which created worry. But I knew worry was not going to add any value and for the second time, decided to stop projecting things that might or might not happen and focus on the facts at hand. The fact was that I was going to a specialist who would provide me with a diagnosis and until I heard from her, all of the thoughts on the subject would be speculation, making them false.

I was busy with my work and family during the days leading up to my visit with Dr T. Keeping busy helped me to avoid dwelling on the mass in my shoulder. When I was tempted to go back to researching, I consciously turned my attention to other more useful and productive activities. Focusing on an unsolvable challenge hurts your process of healing and overcoming. Replacing the fear with a healthy, positive, nurturing and engaging focus is a good way to put your mind on something else for a minute while you're dealing with a tough situation. It not only keeps your focus on productivity, but it also creates space to manage your fear and develop your positive thoughtful approach.

On my way to the hospital to see Dr. T. I fully embraced my typical "remove emotions and deal with the facts to find a solution" posture. It is the proven way of approaching difficult situations without allowing in the emotional turmoil of things that are just in our minds that may or may not exist in.

Turned out that the radiologist misread the MRI and it's just another fatty cyst that can live in my shoulder forever with no impact on my well-being. Go figure. This was just an opportunity to think about my thoughts and gain a few insights. Thank you, God.

It is worth noting that my six days of waiting could have been very different had I given into the initial fear, doubt and worry. We have all hyped situations to dramatic conclusions, often making matters worse while scripting scenarios in our minds, which most often turn out to be false. When we have a choice on how to best think about a topic, the most positive thoughts and words can be intentionally used to support the desired results. It's easier and healthier to listen to your Unique Inner Power than listening to your ego.

The Think About Your Thoughts Worksheet in the Think Again Workbook will enable you to write down your thoughts about everyday life and then to write your thoughts on the thoughts.

Chapter Nine

New Statement Technique

Y*OU MAY NOT GET TO choose how you initially feel, but you do get to choose how you think about your feelings.* Good or bad, positive or negative, happy or sad, energized or deflated, engaged or bored, winner or loser, you choose.

When I ran my business, we were constantly creating new design concepts and presenting to our customers. While rejected designs typically created initial feelings of letdown, we always chose to recognize that design and imagination are subjective, and rejected designs were opportunities to improve upon a foundation. Whenever we missed a first design round, we seamlessly moved straight into the next round, recognizing that creativity is a process of experimentation, interpretation of subjective opinions, and adaptation based on needs of the stakeholders.

I play pickleball on the weekends. While we play hard and are determined to win every game, it is not possible. Even the most elite athletes in the world rarely have perfect records. When we win, we tend to feel naturally exhilarated and congratulate each other with smiles and high fives. But when we lose, we often feel let down initially. Then we take the bad feeling and pat ourselves on the back for playing hard and putting everything we had into every point, and we ultimately remind ourselves how much fun we have playing the game. Yes, we are very competitive! The smile may be a moment delayed, but the intentional thought of appreciation kicks in quickly after victory and defeat. These thoughts are choices that we make, soon after the feelings of victory or defeat set in, and in so doing, our conversations remain positive and friendship opportunities beyond the game continue to develop.

Circumstance and your initial reactive feelings are largely influenced by your worldview and often beyond your control at the point of your experience with the feelings. Your second line of defense—your thoughts on your feelings—is entirely within your control. I know this is hard to believe, but you are in a position to craft each and every thought in life to align with your Unique IP with a goal of feeling and acting like your best self in response to every feeling you experience.

Could you take those stories or comments from your thoughts and write new stories to replace the ones that are holding you back?

You bet. You just need an effective tool up for the challenge. The right tool will help you take action to yield a new result whenever your awareness meets your particular challenge. Your ability to implement the tool and desire to follow through consistently until your new reality replaces the previous reality is key to your success. Changing emotion, feeling, and behavior takes time and dedication; do not rush the results. If you commit to replacing all the unwanted thoughts, words, and actions over the next six months, then you will have plenty of time to make a big impact on your life.

This is not a suggestion that you ignore feelings of sadness, loneliness, or other feelings that might bring you down. There is a time for mourning and for purposefully allowing yourself to feel your emotions. But if your emotions and the thoughts that surround them are not contributing to a positive progression in your life, you need to declare your intention to feel good. You might also consider a deadline to begin the shift in thinking on the topic that has you down. This will give you time to understand the thoughts you have around your feelings and to listen to the words you are speaking about those feelings. When your deadline is up, you will need to begin to think about new thoughts that will replace the existing thoughts and hopefully make you feel better as a result. If someone in your life passes on, give yourself permission to mourn, and then declare when the end of your mourning will occur and how you will change your thoughts at that point. You might go from thinking, "This is so sad, I cannot live without him," to, "I learned so much from him, today I intend to share his lessons with everyone I meet."

The New Statement technique involves creating a simple statement about any belief that is currently holding you back or, more simply, any thought that is not propelling you forward. The new statement that you make will permanently remove and replace previously unproductive thoughts and actions about a specific feeling or topic.

Turn to the Think Again Workbook and find the New Statement Worksheet. All you have to do is identify the unwanted thoughts and statements you make and what triggers those statements and then write that down.

Beside the unwanted statement, write a new replacement statement that helps you remain more in line with your Unique IP when you think and say it. Leave both statements side by side on the worksheet until the process of permanently replacing the old statement with the new statement is complete. At that point, you will erase the old statement, symbolically making it vanish from your thoughts, leaving only the empowering new statement in its place. Continue the process of adding and replacing old statements with new statements.

Eventually, you will have a list of all the statements that represent how you think and speak. This will be a powerful, intentional, and honest document that reminds yourself continuously of your Unique IP.

Let's say that you justify your short fuse with the statement, "It runs in the family." Every time you make this statement, you inform yourself and the people around you of your false beliefs that this is just the way you are and that you are not interested in changing. This statement, of course, is not true. It is just a function of the words that come out of your mouth after you think a false thought about the feelings that trigger your temper.

It may appear to be easier to have everyone accept you just the way you are. But what happens when the way you are is not aligned with who you are meant to be? Then, your actions should not be acceptable to you, even if everyone else has been fooled into thinking it's a done deal. You are absolutely responsible to continuously realign yourself with thoughts, words, and actions that fit with your Unique IP. You owe it to yourself first and foremost, but *the people around you will be pleasantly surprised and happier to be with you when you change your limiting beliefs about yourself to limitless beliefs.*

So, the question is, who do you want to be? The person with the short fuse or the person with the patience? Patience comes from your intentional strategy to align with love, compassion, and care. The short fuse would originate from intolerance, ignorance, and fear. You get to choose. Start by writing yourself a new statement: "When my temper is triggered, I commit to being patient."

How you align your baseline thinking will determine your worldview and become the largest influencer of your emotions and feelings.

> You can condition your emotional reactions to circumstance by removing alignments with fear, doubt, and worry and creating alignments with love, God, kindness, and humanity.

These worldview alignments require you to see all things through the eyes of God. By doing so, emotions and feelings that are ordinarily reacting and "out of your control" are created to support your Unique IP. With feelings of love, thoughts and words of love will come naturally. It is largely the feelings and emotions that we have not conditioned that negatively impact our thoughts.

In addition to new statements about your feelings and emotions, you will need to examine the conditioning you are setting for your feelings. Your worldviews are the spiritual principles you silently acknowledge in conjunction with your Unique IP. You might, for example, possess expansive beliefs:
- God is our creator.
- God is omnipresent.
- When I need truth, I look within.
- I strive to speak only words of love.
- All of humanity are my brothers and sisters.

Alternatively, you might live with limiting beliefs:
- Science alone created the universe.
- Social classes are part of the natural order.
- Racism is acceptable.
- Life is a competition.
- Revenge is required.

Many believe that we have no control over emotions and feelings. But I contend that your feelings and emotions are informed by your worldview on humanity, equality, society, creation, fear, doubt, worry, love, and hate. Before you begin work on your New Statement Worksheet, create a Worldview Worksheet (also in the Think Again Workbook) and be brutally honest with yourself about how you see it. Consider whether your worldviews are aligned with your Unique IP.

The best way to develop a new habit is to practice. As you practice your new statement, you will develop muscle memory in your brain. The triggers that used to activate unwanted thoughts and words will soon activate the new, improved, wanted, healthy, healing thoughts and words. This might not feel natural, but neither did riding a bike or walking at first try. Most of you practiced each of these things over and over again before they became automatic activities that, once mastered, no longer required preparation to execute. The new habits you form will train your mind to think per your instruction. With your guidance and practice, your mind will think with your new statement, just as you trained your body to balance on a bike while peddling and your feet to balance your body while stepping.

If you write down and read your new statement three to five times a day for 45 days, you will create a new habit and permanently change your behavior on the subject at hand to manifest your new reality. Frequently reading the statement allows you to remember it either immediately before or after each time the challenging situation arises. Keep the statement in your possession and it will build awareness until one day, your words will follow your thoughts and the results will be, in the example above, patience. Make a few copies: one for your wallet, one for your desk, and one to keep on your nightstand. This way, your new statement will always be nearby.

> The challenging issues that trigger and impact most people are nuances of life from past experience.

To compound the problem, people live in fear of repeating a similar experience. Both past and future worry impact your present moments, in which, in a perfect world, we should not be concerned with what happened before or what might or might not happen in the future.

For example, imagine that you were told by a teacher in your childhood that you weren't smart enough and would never amount to anything. This might subconsciously trigger feelings and thoughts of resentment when your boss or someone else is providing constructive criticism with the intent to help you improve. While the intent of your boss might be in your best interest and delivered in the kindest manner, you might lump statements being made on your performance with the idea that you are not smart enough. Although the two instances of criticism are very different, the line between destructive and constructive criticism is often blurred and can be a source of confusion. In this example, instead of receiving the information with appreciation, you are triggered to think thoughts of resentment toward your boss, and somewhere deep inside, you tell yourself that he/she doesn't think you are smart enough to do your job. Sometimes subconscious thoughts remind us of things that we may or may not even remember, but they cause us to think and act in ways that are counterproductive to leading a loving, productive, happy life.

The positive experiences of the past tend to enhance our confidence in the present and propel us, while the negative experiences from the past tend to hold us back, until we are aware of them and decide to take alternative action.

It is not the experiences of our past that are responsible for our actions being taken today. Instead, it is our present awareness, perception, thoughts, resulting words, and, finally, our actions. Our ability to constantly recreate how we think about like topics impacts how successful we are at moving forward.

When we see our present thoughts on a topic, we can be informed whether those thoughts are influenced by positive or negative experiences from the past. In your awareness, you will convert the positive memories to good feelings and the negative memories will need to be re-imagined in a new and powerful way. The negative memories will be added to your trigger list so that you can identify the old destructive statements associated with the memory and garner your new statement to improve your life forever.

Your willingness and ability to seek out the things about you that make you great are equally as important to you seeking out the things that challenge your growth.

The Worldview Challenge Worksheet in the Think Again Workbook will enable you to agree or disagree with a series of Worldview statements.

The Worldview Challenge Worksheet and the New Statement Worksheet are simple tools to help you understand what influences your feelings as you change your thoughts and behaviors around challenging topics.

Familiarity is a compounding effect that causes us to repeat mistakes. The longer you live with ego thoughts, including defense mechanisms, bad habits, and sometimes survival mechanisms, the more comfortable you become with them. Even if you know that the thoughts, words, and actions that follow are counterproductive, you master the thoughts, know how to speak about them with authority, and learn how to cope with the consequences. While the thoughts yield undesirable results and do not move you toward realignment, you continue your complacent thinking, mostly due to familiarity.

You cannot confuse familiarity with awareness. They oppose each other in this situation. Just because you know how to do something does not mean you should continue to do it. Awareness of how the thoughts you think, words you speak, and things you do align with your Unique IP is central to your happiness. It takes hard work and time to produce meaningful change.

In order to simplify the process of course correcting your life, the New Statement technique can be an effective tool. It is not required of the New Statement technique to contemplate the past in order to be effective. If you want to do a deep dive, try to recall the past source of your fear, doubt, worry, anger, or resentment. But if that's too deep or difficult, just be present and deal with the facts in front of you.

You can start by looking at the most recent action you took that you were not proud of and wish you could have changed. While you cannot change what you did, you can change what you intend to do the next time. Examine what triggered you to behave poorly. Recall and list your thoughts, words, and actions that made you and other people feel badly.

If this is going to work, you need to be brutally honest with yourself. In order to be brutally honest and for this critical exercise to help you, you will have to let go of some false beliefs. False beliefs include statements that you make to excuse your thoughts, words, and actions. The ego thoughts used to justify your actions and explain yourself. Instead of trying to justify yourself, you will need to examine why the false beliefs perpetuate and prevent you from looking at and seeing yourself honestly. Here is a list of some common false belief statements:

> "You make me sad."
> "I am like this because my father was like this."
> "This is just what God wanted for me."
> "This is the best I can do."
> "The job causes stress."
> "My kids are out of control."
> "My boss is a jerk."
> "My career is a mess."
> "I have no control of the situation."

Get the picture? Can you think of a few limiting thoughts that get in your way? If you can, start writing them down.

If you have false beliefs, remember that you created the thoughts and you can recreate them at any time. Consider the opposite thought to the one you are having and listen to what it sounds like. Restate the thought as many times as you need to until you hear something that resonates with your Unique IP and aligns you with who you know yourself to be. While your thoughts might have been born as a result of events in your life, they now belong to you. They also might have originated in your subconscious mind.

The subconscious is the part of the mind that is not currently in focal awareness. The word "subconscious" was coined by the psychologist Pierre Janet (1859-1947), who argued that underneath the layers of critical-thought functions of the conscious mind lay a powerful awareness that he called the "subconscious mind." Sigmund Freud first used the term "subconscious" in 1893 to describe associations and impulses that are not accessible to consciousness. He later abandoned the term in favor of "unconscious," but for our purposes, we will use the word "subconscious."

The conscious mind includes such things as the sensations, perceptions, memories, feelings, and fantasies inside of our current awareness. Closely allied with the conscious mind is the preconscious, which includes the things that we are not thinking of at the moment but which we can easily draw into conscious awareness. Your ability to recognize subconscious thought in your conscious mind will be relevant to your growth.

Your thoughts are triggered by your feelings and inform your words. Your words inform the people in your life of who you are. Your words tell people how to treat you, what you expect of them, and what they can expect of you. When you set clear expectations, the results you get tend to align with what you asked for. Are all of your results aligned with your Unique IP? Are any of your results aligned with your non-source power or ego? Are you aware of your deepest thoughts? Have you explored subconscious, preconscious, and conscious thoughts? If the thoughts align and make you feel good, go at it. If they are causing problems for you, get yourself ready to change.

Below is an example of what a New Statement Worksheet will look like. Your blank worksheet can be found in the Think Again Workbook.

What Triggers Me	Old Statement	New Statement
1. I am asked to help someone with a task.	I am consumed with work and too busy for anything else.	When meaningful people in my life need me, I make myself available.
2. Employee is not accomplishing tasks quickly enough.	When people are not succeeding, it must be that they are lazy.	When someone is having a challenge, I take the time to listen to the true source of his or her challenge and provide non-judgmental insight.
3. Spouse contradicts me with my children.	My spouse has no respect for my parenting direction.	When I feel disrespected, I will ask my spouse how we can be better aligned to provide love and security for our children.
4. People misunderstand me.	You need to listen better when I speak.	I need to take my time and communicate more clearly.

The idea of creating a new statement recognizes that it is not enough to simply stop unwanted thoughts and actions.

If you remove the unwanted thought without a replacement, the unwanted thought will, by default, be your only thought when the trigger of your topic shows up again.

You must replace the unwanted thoughts and actions with new and better ones. You will replace your short temper with patience. You might replace drinking too much alcohol with drinking water. You can substitute toxic relationships with love-driven friendship. You can replace self-hate with self-love. Replace blame with ownership, negative with positive, sad with happy. New statements are completely up to you. You can work on more than one at a time.

Training your mind to replace old thoughts with new thoughts is the fastest and most direct way to remove and fix your bad habits. You need to realize that your undesirable results have to be replaced and not ignored. The only way to create a new result is to create a new thought. Using the New Statement technique replaces the old thought with a new thought. You cannot just simply remove the old negative thought. It must be replaced with a new, positive one. By continuing your awareness of the old thought but repeating your new statement, every day for 45 days, you will train your brain to listen to the triggers, become aware, think differently on the topic, and create a new reality.

As you are changing, the people around you see the new you, particularly those who were most affected by the old actions. Be aware that this group of people might not believe what they are seeing at first and they might try to convince you that your true thoughts are what they used to be. It is your job to listen to yourself reading your new statement over and over again and to be unwavering in your determination to move the unwanted reactions to your triggers from your life. Don't allow old views of you by others impact the progress you are making to better yourself. When people see your commitment, and your commitment is supported by new actions, they will begin to support the new you. While words matter and set the stage, seeing is believing. As long as your actions follow your words, be prepared to be supported by those around you as you implement your new behaviors.

> Like it or not, ego thoughts are always viable. These are the thoughts that made it into your IP by mistake that need to be removed and replaced.

If you take an honest look at your likes and dislikes about yourself, you will find that the list of dislikes are ego-based thoughts that originated from the outside, infiltrated, and manifested into your reality. Unbeknownst to you, due to lack of awareness, the unwanted ideas accidentally entered your consciousness. Left unchecked, these thoughts turned into words and actions. Your words and actions attracted support for the negative thoughts and there you were, in the wrong game, with the wrong people, misaligned and unhappy. This is how you arrive in the wrong relationship, job, self-image, life view, or direction. The fact that you have taken misaligned paths to places you don't belong is not permanent and does not limit you to remaining out of sync with your Unique IP. Take control and fix the parts of your life that aren't working. There is a way to use ego thoughts productively, but only if you learn to enhance your awareness, listen to your thoughts as you think them, learn to identify the ego thoughts as they creep into your thought process, and then stop them in their tracks and observe them for what they are.

The New Statement technique is the tool you will use to remove and replace the ego thoughts that found their way into your precious mind space. You will need to forgive yourself for anyone you offended or hurt. You not only need to forgive yourself, but you need to practice self-acceptance for who you will be once you move on. Further, accept yourself as is, where you are at each moment of your growth process. This may be who you were, but not who you are. The act of authentically asking for forgiveness is all you need to do to open the doorway to redemption, clarification, and new possibilities. When the door opens, proactively proceed with the removal of invasive, unwanted thoughts that stand in your way. Replace them with positive, powerful, God-given Inner Power thoughts and watch your life blossom in new directions.

> *"What lies behind us and what lies before us are tiny matters compared to what lies within us."*
> – RALPH WALDO EMERSON

Inner Power can be overridden or smothered by ego but cannot be removed under any circumstance. It will become bigger, better, and more powerful as you develop as a fully realized spiritual human being. You may ignore your Unique IP or simply not realize that you own it. But rest assured, it's there, it's yours, and it's powerful enough to propel you into your fully realized magnificent self.

Chapter Ten

Communicate

R ECOGNIZING THAT YOU ARE UNIQUE unto yourself will draw you to the conclusion that you have special gifts to deliver to the world. When you identify and associate with those who are developing their unique gifts, you realize that everyone brings value to the world in their own individualized way.

Unique Inner Power is universally described as your purpose for being alive that, when understood and developed, opens your life to exponential love and abundance.

This is a way of being, a skill, an activity, or something else that you would do with love in your heart whether or not you were being paid, observed, or otherwise acknowledged. You do it when no one is watching simply because it's what you do. I asked my seven-year-old son how he knows how to dance as if he's had 20 years of training. He replied, "I feel it from the inside, I just know." And that's what it's like to acknowledge, embrace, trust, and implement on Unique IP.

Developing our Inner Power happens when we align ourselves with the God-given talents that were in our possession when we were delivered to life. When you align with God, you might say, "To know me is to know God." You might be so bold to say, "I am God," because in reality, when you are a piece of what God made, you are part of God, and therefore you are God. Knowing your Unique IP is knowing the most special part(s) of yourself. Children have an easier time knowing and trusting God, particularly when their awareness is nurtured, communicated with, and supported. But either way, you will spend most of your life finding and knowing God inside of you, developing the gifts that already exist, finding those that don't exist yet, and converting unhealthy, unwanted outside influence.

Not all outside influence is bad. So much outside influence is positive, supports our Unique IP in perfect harmony, and deserves to be interpreted and integrated with who we are. *Since we all have uniquely distinct talents and gifts, we need each other to collaborate and realize our greatest potential.* Each of us brings a unique approach to each and every part of life. By collaborating with others, you recognize all other gifts that need to be present to achieve your vision. Stay in your lane by focusing on your greatest Unique Inner Powers while collaborating with people whose Unique IP is able to contribute to manifesting your vision. By collaborating, you will achieve your vision without trying to be someone who you are not. You will also avoid the temptations of outside ego thoughts by being more in sync with aligned thinkers. The same way you collaborate with people to achieve your own vision, you will also collaborate with people to help them achieve theirs. *The most powerful way to develop as a human being is to give away the things that you value most to people who need them most.* In return, people will collaborate with you and give away the things that they value most to you when you are in need.

Giving and receiving is a transfer of energy that comes back to your life in amounts equal to the energy you deliver. The person you give to might not be the person who gives back. It is the act of giving with no expectations of reciprocity that gives you credit. The return may come from a place that you least expect, but trust and know, it will come. Since energy is energy, the rule applies to both positive Unique IP energy as well as ego energy.

What you give is what you get. Hence, if you are not getting what you want, think about what you are giving.

The Giving Worksheet in the Think Again Workbook will enable you to write down 10 things you receive from people in your life and from life itself. All things that are notable, whether good or bad. You will further list the things you know you give that contribute to what you are receiving.

Start with appreciating the unique offerings that people around you bring to the world. Give them all that you have that will add value and joy to their lives, no strings attached. Tell people that you appreciate them. What you receive in return will produce personal spiritual growth for you and, in turn, for the people in your life.

Chapter Eleven

Remember God

It's easy to lose your way as you journey through the day-to-day rhythms of life. Reminding yourself of the power of God is essential, especially if you are out of sync with your Inner Power. Reflections on the journey will bring you all the way back to your birth and childhood, where you knew God most intimately and most authentically. When I was young, I knew God. But then, with time and unfiltered influence from the outside world, I lost my way.

> *"Do not go where the path may lead, go instead where there is no path and leave a trail."*
> – *Ralph Waldo Emerson*

After my first 20 years on a clear spiritual path, I started on an unaware path that gradually took me so far from my Inner Power that when asked at age 30, "Do you believe in God," I was dumbfounded when I could not answer. That was the day I started on my journey home, in search of God and my missing Unique Inner Power. While the influencers in my life were well intentioned, loving, and caring, they were not without flaws. My self-awareness was powerful from my earliest memory, but as I grew up being bullied by schoolmates and misguided by family members, I somewhere lost my sense of Unique IP and began to assimilate in ordinary ways that detached me from my purpose.

Although I had deviated far from my Unique IP, I found my way home one step at a time with the spiritual guidance of two great men, Steve D'Annunzio, founder of Soul Purpose Institute and spiritual advisor to thousands of successful business men and women, and Dr. Wayne Dyer, the acclaimed Hay House author who sold over 25 million books. They reminded me that I was in control of the conditions, thoughts, and actions in my life. I had developed defense mechanisms that helped me to manage the challenges of my childhood and young adult years. By the time these defenses were no longer necessary, I had allowed many false beliefs and ego thoughts to the inside. I was in a difficult position, needing to identify and separate with unwanted thoughts from Unique IP. I realized that while dealing with the bullies, I developed a series of false beliefs that would help me get through that period of time, but those beliefs were no longer useful and had to be removed and replaced. My mentors led me to reclaim myself by filtering my thoughts through the eyes of God and trusting the intangible infinite power that I possessed.

> You have the ability to think about your thoughts and choose the ones that make you healthy and whole.

If you choose positive, powerful thoughts, you will be strengthened. To the contrary, negative thoughts will weaken you and lead to destruction. Remember, all thoughts filter through you, including the thoughts that belong to other people. You can repeat someone else's thought, but you cannot own another's thought until you successfully filter it through your Unique IP, hence taking full and complete ownership of the thought from your unique perspective.

When I was a student at Boston University, a friend's parent asked me what I wanted to do after graduation. My immature reply was that I wanted to make a lot of money. I went into the commercial real estate business. As a broker, within a few years, I indeed was making a lot of money. A few years after that, I was asked a similar question by my close friend in the commercial real estate business. She asked what I really wanted to do with myself. I told her that I mostly wanted to be happy. I believed that making money should be a byproduct of work that was meaningful. On that day, I listened to my inner calling and knew that my creativity and innate capabilities would drive my thoughts of family, career, and income for the rest of my life. Love and creativity were at the core of my Unique IP, my calling, and my vision. Finally, I found the courage to acknowledge myself as capable and deserving to pursue my passion.

> *"The teacher who is indeed wise*
> *does not bid you to enter the house*
> *of his wisdom but rather leads you*
> *to the threshold of your mind."*
> — KHALIL GIBRAN

When the student is ready, the teacher appears. The truth is that the answers to your questions are usually right inside of you. You are the student. God, often through others and sometimes through your very self, is the teacher. The answers live within your Inner Power. But until we are ready to acknowledge our power and to do something about it, the doors to opportunity stay locked inside. This often causes a real frustration, knowing something is so close, yet seemingly unattainable. You yourself are holding the key to unlock the door. Think of it like this: you have a giant key ring with lots of keys on it. But you use the same few keys over and over again, while the majority of the keys on the ring go unused. Some may be old keys to old doors that you don't want or need to walk through anymore. Others are brand new keys that you haven't tried out yet. Those new keys will work when you are ready to simply place them in the new keyhole and turn. Until then, remember they are in your pocket.

> *"Your pain is the breaking of the shell
> that encloses your understanding."*
> – KHALIL GIBRAN

When you come face to face with your Unique IP, you own the greatest opportunity of your life to unlock the biggest door to your new and improved life and to collaborate with people who have abilities in sync with your vision. The decision, as always, is yours.

Chapter Twelve

Forgive

UNJUSTIFIED GRUDGES AND RESENTMENTS ARE a great source of your internal unrest. The funny thing about a grudge or resentment is that the subject of your angst is unaffected by the internal misalignment affecting your behavior. When we hold onto hostility and anger, the damaging feelings keep us bound to the past wallowing in emotional pain. Forgiveness is the gift that we give to ourselves to heal ourselves.

If you believe the person who offended you did the best that they could with the tools that they had at the time of the offense, then forgiveness will come easy.

If you allow your ego to win, you will say he knew better and should have done better. With this thought process, you might remain angry and feel that the issue is unresolved. There are no facts about your feelings, just opinions that are neither true nor false. If God were in the room, God might have you say about the unpleasant action, "I know you did your best. I love and forgive you."

Forgiveness is a strong way to feed and develop your Unique IP. It is your way of managing an emotion-based thought in a positive way. When you forgive, you give up hope that the past should have been different. You recognize that you cannot change what happened. You gain awareness that reliving past pain in your present moments of reflection hinders your ability to be present with people and places in your life today. When we hold onto the pain, we live in the past, making it virtually impossible to move forward.

> *"The practice of forgiveness is our most important contribution to the healing of the world."*
> — MARIANNE WILLIAMSON

Months before my father passed away, my older brother threw me out of the family business. My father had been coaching us on improving our relationship for months leading up to my brother's action. While I was shocked at my brother's behavior, I was most upset that my father allowed himself to be manipulated into supporting the action. While the decision for us to separate had merit and was the subject of many hours of deep discussion, I always expected the outcome to be driven by love and appreciation. Instead, the plan that passed was driven by ego based on my brother's fear, doubt, and worry. He shared with me years later that he thought I was planning to leave the company and steal the business. While this was never my plan and was not true, he allowed his ego to think it, develop a false narrative, talk about it, turn it into reality, and contribute direly in the destruction of our family.

Unfortunately, I held the false belief that my father could have stopped my brother from taking the fearful actions to end our business partnership that changed our family forever. As I listened to my own ego support my anger over the belief that my father should have stepped in, my father passed away. As a result of my inability to forgive, my father and I left each other, governed by our ego-thinking minds stuck in doubt, unhappiness, and disappointment. This was a tough pill to swallow after a lifetime of love, mutual respect, and deep bonds. There was no way to turn back time or properly, lovingly, and rightfully forgive him before he passed. He was already gone. It is often such unrealistic expectations that cause us so much pain.

The sad thing in retrospect was that I made a mistake listening to my ego instead of listening to my Unique IP. My inner voice knew that I had to forgive my father and give him all my love, especially in his greatest time of need. Instead, I allowed my ego to convince me that my resentments were justified and that I was right to be angry.

Only when I let go of the ego thoughts and let God guide me did I come to terms that he did the best he could do at the time with the tools that he had. Eventually, my love for my father filled me again as it did before the incident. It took me a long time to forgive myself for not forgiving my father before he passed.

The Forgiveness Worksheet in the Think Again Workbook will enable you to write down 10 grudges or resentments that you hold and the people (including yourself) that you forgive.

> *"If you change the way you look at things, the things you look at change."*
> – Dr. Wayne Dyer

Chapter Thirteen

Flow

UNEXPECTED THINGS STAND IN OUR way all the time. *Sometimes the very things that we think are in our way are there to teach us flexibility and guide us to the safety of our destiny.* Success is sometimes disguised in the most mysterious ways. How many entrepreneurs and inventors tell the similar story of the multiple failures that were required to get to the one big success? Einstein described his years failing to invent electricity as the time it took to learn enough lessons to get it right. Failure is positive when it is looked at as an often necessary part of the process to achieve a desired result.

The most successful people in the world are not necessarily the most intelligent.

> *The most successful people are those who are most resilient and adaptable. Those who flow like water can read people, situations, and life.*

They take their cues from their inner and external environments and then make modifications, aligned with

Unique Inner Power, to adapt. They have a clear and decisive point of view on who they are and how they behave in the world, but they are flexible. *They are so certain on who they want to be in the future that their awareness of who they actually are right now is heightened and triggers adjustments every day.*

Think of Tony Dorsett, one of the greatest football running backs of all time who played for the Dallas Cowboys. He would go to the huddle and receive a play to run straight up the middle between the center and the left guard. As the quarterback handed him the ball, if Dorsett saw the linebacker from the opposing team standing exactly in his planned route, he intuitively modified his route on the fly, cut left to an opening, gaining yardage and moving closer to the ultimate goal of scoring. The difference between the good running backs and the great ones has a lot to do with their ability to flow like water, modify the plan, and adapt to the present moment reality.

> *"When you start to walk out of
> the way, the way appears."*
>
> – *Rumi*

The following poem, "Flow Like Water," came about as I imagined a drop of water flowing down the Hudson River, past Manhattan, on the way to the Atlantic Ocean. When the drop of water flowed into a boulder on the river bank at its origin way upstate New York, it simply rolled off and continued on its journey. The illustration emphasizes our need to be clear on our direction, but adaptable when unexpected interruptions push us off course. I wrote this poem, inspired by the story.

Flow Like Water

Flow like water
Find God at your bedside when you wake
Put your hand on your heart
Thankful for the breath you take
Flow like water
Blow a cool breeze from your lips through the room
Smile with appreciation
Pour love on fear and doubt
Shower hope on worry
Be open to accept whatever you did not expect
Flow like water
Step outside each day with confidence
Be a force of nature
Be a force of God
Be soft and vulnerable like a flower
Be kind and powerful
Flow like water
Forgive the ones who sleepwalk through your path
Be bold when passion calls your name
Choose love
Flow like water
Listen to your soul
Shed tears of joy and sorrow
Fill your heart with music
Close your eyes and dance
Flow like water
Be inspired by a look in someone's eyes
Know God
Give away the things you value most

Protect your family, hold them close
Learn to listen, learn to learn
Know the joy of teaching
Flow like water
Remember God
Be your most glorious self now
Choose love
Flow like water

You face the challenges of life every day. Challenges come to all people from all places. The challenges we typically face fall into one of four categories: economic, health, faith, and relationship. Regardless of the category or the specifics of the challenge, *your success lies in your ability to wake up in the morning, pray, appreciate, put your feet on the ground, and approach the day with a deliberate intention to turn your biggest challenges into your greatest solutions.*

Your ability to be in charge of your day is critical to managing your best life. Being in charge requires a game plan with strategies to implement the plan. *On a day-to-day basis, you are running ideas that support the strategy for the overall plan.*

When you make mistakes, it is your responsibility to be accepting, forgive yourself, and course correct to get back on track with your strategy.

In golf, the golfer is taught to focus on one shot at a time. Inside of each shot is routine, posture, swing, technique, balance, and focus. The golfer thinking about his last shot, or his next shot, or the activity of his opponent will inevitably fail. Being inwardly focused and present is central to being successful. In the present, we are focused on right now with a clear stream of consciousness.

Chapter Fourteen

Compassion

A FATHER AND THREE CHILDREN STEPPED onto a train to travel home after a very long day. The children were unruly, yelling, jumping, and disturbing the passengers. Many of the passengers were looking at the father in disbelief that he was standing by taking no action with his poorly behaved children. He sat hunched over, head in hands, gazing at the floor of the train. Finally, a woman approached him and forcefully said, "Do something about your children!" He looked up, suddenly noticed his children, gazed back at the woman with tears in his eyes and said, "I am so sorry, we just came from the hospital. Their mother passed away today. This is not their normal behavior. Please forgive us."

> "When you judge another, you do not
> define them, you define yourself."
> – Dr. Wayne Dyer

Filter your judgments through the eyes of God and know that people are inherently good. *When God's goodness is not shining through, your compassion is required.*

The opportunity to deliver love in response to someone out of sync with the universe is a gift for you to recognize and act upon.

You were born with the ability to put yourself in someone else's shoes and to see and feel from their perspective. *When you see your needs without consideration of another's, you are out of sync with the core essence of human compassion.* From the time my daughter Grace was five years old, she has been able to intuitively know when others are out of sync. She will say things like, "Are you okay, you don't seem like yourself," or, "Do you need to talk?" when she feels the need to raise your awareness. Her questions provide a selfless, optimistic understanding. She listens to the answers and usually provides helpful insight. She is now 11 years old and lives in a forgiving, non-judgmental space, typically giving others the benefit of the doubt.

As you journey back to God, try to remember the grace in you and how you have cared deeply about people in your life from your earliest memories. This is who you are inside. Your ability to reconnect will be great progress to getting in sync with your source.

> *"It is not our purpose to become each other;*
> *it is to recognize each other, to learn to see*
> *the other and honor him for what he is."*
> — *Herman Hesse*

Chapter Fifteen

Listen

*"The number one thing people
crave is to be heard."*
— Oprah Winfrey

When you listen with your heart and soul, you listen more deeply and insightfully than just listening with your ears. When you can listen from your heart, you open doors in your relationships wider, allowing the full abundance of available light and love to shine through. When you listen like this, the people you listen to will feel truly heard.

*"The quieter you become the
more you can hear."*
— Ram Dass

Sometimes, listening is about seeking out people who know more than you do. Sometimes, listening is about connecting your heart with someone who needs to be heard. Other times, it is about your need to listen to yourself and to no one else.

When you have a special inner knowing, listening to others might influence your new and ingenious ideas and perhaps stifle them and change the course of your destiny. When you have an innate knowing about a subject matter, it is best to first fully develop and express yourself with no outside influence. Trust yourself and be fearless to try out your idea prior to opening your mind to outside influence. It is okay to flat out reject conventional thoughts through your source filter if they are not in sync with your vision.

When you have fully developed your point of view, only then should you consider learning how other people have tackled your topic before you, if they have at all. Fully developing the idea includes thinking, speaking, and acting on your ideas. As you bring your words and actions into the world, you will receive direct feedback. With each response you receive, you will evolve your unique point of view. Your awareness of who you are receiving feedback from will give you direct context to the relevance of the information. Remember that each person on Earth has their own unique experience and therefore their own opinions on each and every subject matter presented. It is up to you to decide whether their feedback is relevant to you in the context of their unique perspective.

Unique perspective and individual experience are the trickiest parts of communicating with other human beings. *Since we only know the full and complete story of our own individual life, it is virtually impossible to fully understand where someone else is coming from.* For example, if you are discussing *Roe vs. Wade* with a woman who has a personal experience with abortion, she will have a unique perspective, possibly unlike anyone else. Unless she shared her story with you, you would not know what shaped her point of view. If you asked whether she supported a woman's right to choose, she might just say, "Yes, of course." Without hearing her experience, you would just know the end result of a complex thought process that led to her ultimate conclusion of support. Whatever your thoughts are on this topic, your ability to use her opinion in a productive way is limited to your insight of her full and complete story.

In a simpler example, did you ever wonder why you ask the waitress for a recommendation when trying to decide what to order for dinner? Without context of the type of foods she likes and dislikes, you will not be able to evaluate and compare her taste buds to your own and the recommendation would be largely irrelevant.

The most advanced listeners are the strongest and most accurate questioners. Asking questions of people provides you the opportunity to receive critical data that will position you to understand their subsequent words and actions. Our experiences shape our perspective of the world. All of your words come directly from your thoughts. *If it's coming out of your mouth, you thought it first.* We are not attempting to judge people, but we are trying to understand whether their thoughts should be allowed entry into our personal inner thought space. It is important to note that not all thoughts that are out of alignment should be filtered out. Sometimes, contrary thoughts can add value, provided that we are aware enough to know that the thought doesn't always align with our Unique IP. A specific thought might be worth holding in a special internal category that you might call your "context" category. The context category can be a reminder of the ego view that you can use to more fully develop your God view. As long as you can draw a clean line between your God thoughts and your context thoughts, these context thoughts can add a valuable layer of perspective to your life.

> *"With everything that has happened to you, you can either feel sorry for yourself or treat what happened as a gift. Everything is either an opportunity to grow or an obstacle to keep you from growing. You get to choose."*
> — Dr. Wayne Dyer

Chapter Sixteen

Just Breathe

THE BRAIN IS ONE OF the largest and most complex organs in the human body. It is made up of more than 100 billion nerves that communicate in trillions of connections called synapses. The brain is made up of many specialized areas that work together.

The brain is an amazing three-pound organ that controls all functions of the body, interprets information from the outside world and embodies the essence of the mind and soul. Intelligence, creativity, emotion, and memory are a few of the many things governed by the brain. Protected within the skull, the brain is composed of the cerebrum, cerebellum, and brainstem.

The brain receives information through our five senses: sight, smell, touch, taste, and hearing. It assembles the messages in a way that has meaning for us, and stores that information in our memory. The brain is the central control for our thoughts, memory and speech, movement of the arms and legs, and the function of many organs within our body.

You might think of you brain as your body's own personal computer. When the computer has too many programs open at the same time, it has a tendency to overload and freeze, requiring the user to shut down and restart. Your brain functions in a similar way. Today, more than ever, your brain experiences information overload on a regular basis.

At any given moment our brain produces thoughts of past, present, future, fear, doubt, worry, to do lists, responsibilities, physical, emotional and the unending supply of information from the outside. No wonder why most of us need to regularly press the reset button. All of these thoughts happening simultaneously in our minds often result in an overwhelming and in some cases paralyzing state, where moving forward becomes a great challenge. When our thoughts are neither organized nor properly processed, the quality of our thinking and decision-making decreases, wasting energy and lowering productivity. When our brains are overloaded, the lines between our inner and outer worlds blur.

Without solid tools to build a better life, some of us turn to ego driven solutions such as drugs, alcohol, excessive work, gambling, negative thoughts and words or anything else that will dull our attention from the misdirected inner dialogues. Ego voices can eventually over-rule love and convince us to accept and give up the fight for freedom and alignment with Unique IP.

Meditation is a practice where an individual uses a technique to achieve a mentally clear and emotionally calm and stable state. Meditation does not mean absence of thought, nor does it mean turning our brain off.

While there are other types of meditation, below are the most commonly used and easy to access at home on your own time.

1. Loving-kindness meditation's goal is to cultivate an attitude of love and kindness toward everything, even your enemies and sources of stress. While breathing deeply, you open your mind to receiving loving kindness. You then send messages of loving kindness to the world, to specific people, or to their loved ones. It can help you manage unjustified anger, frustration, resentment and interpersonal conflict.
2. Mindfulness meditation is a form of meditation that urges you to remain aware and present in the moment. Rather than dwelling on the past or dreading the future, mindfulness encourages awareness of a person's existing surroundings. Lack of judgment is central to this practice, so rather than being annoyed or angry about something, you simply note that it exists without assigning meaning. Mindfulness can reduce fixation on negative emotions, improve focus, improve memory, lessen impulsive, emotional reactions and improve relationship satisfaction.
3. Breath awareness meditation is a type of mindful meditation that encourages mindful breathing. You breathe slowly and deeply, counting your breaths or otherwise focusing on your breaths. The goal is to focus only on breathing and to ignore other thoughts that enter the mind. Breath awareness will help to reduce anxiety, improve concentration, and develop emotional flexibility.
4. Trancendental Meditation is a spiritual form of meditation where you remain seated and breathe

slowly. The goal is to transcend or rise above your current state of being. Practitioners focus on a mantra which can be based on the year one was born or perhaps a statement like "I am good enough" while meditating.

Focusing on your breath is a consistent part of most meditation practices and used to strengthen the muscle in your mind that helps you choose where to give attention.

Most of the time your breathing pattern is shallow, unconscious, involuntary and without a sense of purpose. When you turn your focus to purposeful voluntary breathing, many of the extraordinary results noted above will be produced. The same brain muscle that keeps bringing focus to your breath is the muscle that will help you focus on things of your choice going forward.

The following breath awareness mediation instructional and observations are from Joe Singer, a personal friend of mine, and a life-long practitioner of breath awareness and other meditations. He says anyone can do this and produce big results:

- Sit with your spine erect and close your eyes.
- Place your hands face up loosely on your thigh
- Close your eyes and tilt your head upward
- Bring your focus to your breath. If your mind wonders (as it certainly will) gently bring your attention back to your breath.
- Take deep purposeful breaths

- Allow yourself to feel lightheaded
- The amount of time really does not matter. In the beginning you should try for 2-4 minutes. Eventually 10-20 minutes... twice a day is a great goal.
- Practice this exercise first thing in the morning and then again in the early afternoon.

Joe says after daily consistent meditation, you will gain awareness over the dialogue that occurs in your mind. Ego thoughts and voices that previously hijacked your thinking will no longer have power over your attention. You will become equipped to recognize and ultimately prevent negative thought patterns that have plagued you in the past as you learn to control the dialogue.

Following consistent meditation, we are increasingly happier, healthier, present, efficient, alert, productive, creative and loving. As a result, your thought process, decision-making and actions you take in your life improve. You will recognize opportunities as well as solutions to problems which before were difficult to see.

Deepak Chopra and Oprah Winfrey deliver a fabulous meditation experience online. You can download the mobile app, 21-Day Meditation Experience for free. This is an easy and wise way to start your meditation practice.

Chapter Seventeen

Hierarchy of Thought

Y<small>OU ARE YOUR THOUGHTS. W<small>HETHER</small></small> you realize it or not, your worldview is informed by your karmic Unique IP. Feelings are informed by your worldview, and thoughts are choices made about your feelings. Words and actions follow your thoughts. You form thoughts, then opinions, then stories about almost everything in your life. *In other words, your words follow your thoughts and your life follows your words.* Did you ever notice that if you wake up feeling off and then declare to the morning that you feel crappy, when you go out into the world, it's mostly crappy? Dyer says, "You are what you think."

If you think positive thoughts such as, "I appreciate my breath," "What a beautiful day," "I love my family," "I am happy," "I am smart," "I am beautiful," etc., these thoughts inform decisions on how you feel about your life and about your present moment. First you internalize the thought, then you communicate your decisions to the world, and almost immediately the world responds by confirming your words.

To the contrary, when you decided that you were having a crappy day, people who agreed with you were attracted to your words, energy, and story and therefore supported what you had to say, hence reinforcing a negative thought that you yourself created. When word patterns attract like reactions from people thinking similar thoughts, they are known as "Attractor Words." Strong force attractor words are positive source power words that attract positive source power people. Weak force attractor words are negative non-source power words that attract negative non-source power people.

With every statement you make, you have a choice of words to use. According to the second edition of the 20th Volume Oxford English Dictionary, 171,476 English words are currently in use. In modern Chinese, over 370,000 words exist, 90 million Arabic, 100,000 French, and 150,000 Spanish words, to name a few. In short, whatever language you speak, there is no shortage of vocabulary to accurately express yourself. Typically, you choose either positive or negative words. Are you typically interpreting situations in the most positive light or the most negative? We often make judgments based on our past experiences. On illness, you might say, "He/she will get through this and be good," or, "He/she is in trouble and could die." The first position invokes hope while the second invokes fear. The goal is to lift up whomever you are in a conversation with. When you learn that the forecast for your beach day is cloudy, do you say, "We'll have a great day either way," or do you say, "That stinks"? You may want to ask whether your choice of words is going to add or diminish value in your life. Ask whether your choice will attract happy or unhappy people to you. Ask whether it is true. In most cases, your actions will follow your words and, effectively, you will get what you spoke about.

Many thoughts are subconscious that derive from your unaware mind. However, the thoughts are just as real and impactful as your conscious thoughts because our words follow our subconscious thoughts in the exact same way as they follow our conscious ones. Our actions always follow our words. Our actions do not care about or understand the difference between conscious, preconscious, and subconscious thoughts that developed the words.

We like to think of mind control as awareness of thought.

> The more we are aware of our thoughts and where they come from, the better we can choose which thoughts to filter in or out of our precious inner source power thought space.

Hierarchy of Thought

Karmic Unique IP
Worldview
Feelings
Thoughts
Words
Actions

When you find yourself saying things that don't sound right, your inner filter voice should trigger you to rethink your thoughts. For example, if you hear yourself saying, "I'd like to start my own business, but I don't think I'll succeed," you might want to revisit the thought that created those words. The thought might have been, "I am not smart enough," "I do not deserve to create something," or "How will I succeed with so much competition?" If any of this sounds like you, negative thoughts might have penetrated your precious thought space and could be dictating your view. The thoughts come either from your own personal life experience or from an outside source. If the thoughts attach to your experience, you may need to do a deeper dive into the origin. Recognize that you cannot control or change the past, but you can control how you think about the past in the present moment. If the thought was given energy in the past and if the thought was supported by your very actions in the past, then you can decide that enough is enough.

Ask yourself this question: "Is it true that...?" In this example, you would ask, "Is it true that I am not smart enough?" The answer is, "Only if you think it." You can make a decision right here right now to think and speak the new words, "I am smart enough." Tell people that you are smart enough. They will immediately support you because the people who engage in your conversation will believe and reinforce what you are saying. Here are the exact aware-minded positive thoughts—New Statements—to counter each of the above unaware negative thoughts. "I am smart enough," "I deserve to create and build for myself," and "I have a unique perspective that will allow me to compete."

Your mission is to learn to be aware of your thoughts. When you find yourself thinking thoughts that will hold you back, your ego-thinking mind is in charge. *The ego-thinking mind is constantly presenting thoughts to you, often subconsciously, that are grounded in fear, doubt, and worry.* Fear, doubt, and worry are the foundation block requirements for each and every ego-thinking thought.

If you can learn to see and hear the intrusive thoughts as they enter your inner space, then you will have the power to stop them in their tracks. Your words are your second line of defense. If you miss the opportunity to stop or redirect your thought, the likelihood is that the ego thought has made it to the next level: your words. Your words will inform you when this happens because you will, inevitably, speak those thoughts. As soon as you start speaking negative thoughts, your need to create a new statement becomes more urgent. The longer you wait to change the thought, the more negativity you provide to the people around you. If you do not stop and fix this, you will be in active conversations with people supporting and reinforcing your negativity. Your ego-thinking mind will also be defending your new negative position with people who are aligned with source and attempting to raise your awareness. As you dig your heels in, you will have more negative people around you as they flock and fewer positive people as they flee.

It is only your ability to gain awareness of your thoughts that will allow you to gain control of your words and actions. If your thought was "I can't," you are likely in active conversations with people who are supporting why you can't. They are simply agreeing with you and might be thinking that they are comforting you as a friend would. An aware-minded friend would challenge your "I can't" conversation and invite you to consider the thoughts that are triggering the words. But an unaware friend would simply think that the way of friendship is blind support of whatever words were coming their way. In their unconditional support, they would do you an unintentional disservice, potentially reinforce your story, and guide you to the next level of misalignment.

"*I can*" *and* "*I can't*" are contrary ideologies. You will know you are on and "I can" path because this is consistently how you start your sentences. "I can do better." "I can win this account." "I can be a better parent." "I can succeed." "I can change." I can, I can, I can.

Who do you want to be? Whom do you want to be supported by? Which you do you want to present to the world? *Remember, the people in your life are the mirror back to you of you.* Look around and ask yourself whether the people around you represent the best of who you are. They represent your current thoughts about yourself and about the world around you.

The Hierarchy of Thought Worksheet in the Think Again Workbook will enable you to see some of the thoughts that start on the inside and show up on the outside. You can evaluate whether the thoughts are positively or negatively affecting your life.

Your alignment with God is the ultimate guide to truth in your life. Are you consistently speaking words of God? Are you asking yourself, "If God were in the room, what would he or she have me say?" Are you able to see yourself and observe your thoughts as if you were your spirit-self observing your human-self? Do you have the ability to recognize words and actions of the world around you that are out of alignment with your source of creation? Do you believe that we were placed here to love? We each have an opportunity and an obligation to live how the creator intended us to be in the world.

Chapter Eighteen

Appreciate

*Appreciation is the condition that we
set for love to flow into our lives.*

M¥ MENTOR STEVE D'ANNUNZIO TAUGHT me to thank God for waking me every morning, for the people who love me and for the abundance and the challenges that I have in my life. I start the day in appreciation and remind myself all day long to appreciate every person in my path and everything that happens.

> *"Wake at dawn with a winged heart and
> give thanks for another day of loving."*
> – KAHLIL GIBRAN

This simple exercise of setting a deliberate and intentional condition for the day takes only a few seconds. As I step into the day, my awareness is at a heightened level, and instead of looking for problems and excuses, I seek out opportunities, solutions, and reasons to be thankful. The typical return that I receive is a full day of synchronicity in alignment with my Unique IP and people who are attracted to me. When we put appreciation first, our ego gets pushed out of the way.

Another mentor, Dan Sullivan, coaches that appreciation is the key first step to creating abundance and wealth in our lives. *When we enter each relationship in appreciation, we collaborate with like-minded individuals, create value by delivering our unique abilities, and deliver exponential abundance.*

In business and personal relationships, your success comes from adding value to another person's life by delivering your Unique IP to their process. If your Unique IP can help someone else create more value, then you have something to offer. On the other hand, if what you have to offer cannot add value, you need to reevaluate the relationship. Your objective is to choose the right relationships by determining those who will receive the most value by having you in their lives. When you add value, appreciation shows up in your life. When you receive appreciation, you are inspired to improve your skills so that you can continuously deliver more. The more you give, the more appreciation you receive and the stronger your relationships become. Your focus should be on giving your highest and best self for the sake of giving to the relationship. What you receive in return will be the byproduct of giving.

Part of my Unique IP is architectural and spatial awareness, vision for design, and ability to produce sculptural projects in public spaces. There are always young people around on our installations, usually trying to break into the business. I tend to think out loud, partially because hearing my thoughts allows me to vet them more easily than just thinking about them. So, I do both, think about my thoughts and speak my thoughts. Visual people tend to use the phrase "do you see what I'm saying." That's because we want to know if you have any clue about the fantastical visions racing through our minds. When we are working in a live setting, there is a special opportunity to touch and feel the material, see the scale and balance, and listen to the sounds. It's a great moment for anyone interested to actually see what I'm saying. Maybe this unique opportunity to express myself with all of our senses and sensibilities in play is part of my work's appeal to me. As I satisfy a deep, passionate part of my expression, I also have an opportunity to teach people in my space and ultimately bring beauty to the world.

We all have unique personal abilities. Some of you are always there for your friends, for daily chats, constant support, and everyday conversation. Some of you know how to provide spiritual guidance and insight that offers friends an opportunity to think about the thoughts that are guiding their actions. Others of you share social conversations about things you have in common like sports, movies, and other everyday occurrences. There is no right or wrong way to be a friend in the world, as long as you are aligned with God and focused on giving.

Friendships form in the same way that business relationships form: people add value and exchange appreciation with each other. The relationship grows stronger as the trust builds and people in the relationship each get better and better as a result of knowing and collaborating with each other.

Chapter Nineteen

Self-Identity

When you meet someone for the first time and they say, "Tell me about yourself," how do you respond? Do you tell about your inner self or do you tell about your outer self? The real question is, how do you describe who you are to the outside world? Most of us say what we do for a living. I'm a stockbroker, I'm a designer, I'm a housewife, and so on. But when we define ourselves by what we do, if or when what we do goes away, who are we left with? Who you are anywhere is who you are everywhere, and wherever you go, there you are. Unlike your business or your career, the you inside, your spirit-self, is guaranteed to be with you infinitely.

When we define ourselves by who we are inside, we set stronger conditions for stability when things in our lives change.

Your ability to adapt is a key ingredient to your growth and success in every relationship. As you develop your inner voice by aligning with Unique IP, you create a strong, ever-changing but consistent, reliable human experience. This inner part of you builds and strengthens throughout your life, providing you with a strong, growing platform to stand on as the world moves about.

For many years, I ran a business with over two hundred full-time and seasonal employees. My identity was so closely tied to the identity of the company that a threat to the business felt like a personal threat to me. Over time, I learned new ways of associating and identifying with myself and with the company.

I have learned to identify as a spiritual student of life. With my company, I learned to identify as the leader with a collaborative team of experts. The more I developed, the more I gave away the parts of the business that were not aligned with my Unique IP. As a result, I identified almost exclusively with my greatest strengths, which in turn allowed me to deliver bigger value with each interaction. Others were hired with Unique IP in areas of the company that I was not expert. My purpose for being was so closely aligned with my Unique IP that my personal experience became more consistently positive. My Unique IP remains constant and stands alone as the single most positive force in my life. When my business closed, fortunately, I did not lose everything. I still had myself, my family, friends, my unique relationship with the universe, and most of all, my stable, personal Unique IP identity.

The Self-Identity Worksheet in the Think Again Workbook will enable you to write down 10 statements you make about yourself to determine whether the statements are part of your inner world or part of your outer world.

Chapter Twenty

Ripples

EVERYONE IN THE WORLD HAS the capacity to experience love, wholeness, and peace in their hearts. This is not always apparent or believable in the face of misaligned evil actions and ego thoughts coming at us from everywhere.

> *"I alone cannot change the world, but I can cast a stone across the waters to create many ripples."*
> — MOTHER TERESA

When you examine the people in the world best positioned to deliver and vibrate love to the rest of the world, you realize that if we do this together, we have a good chance at reaching everyone as humanity merges toward a higher state of consciousness. With time, patience, and faith, love will win.

We will form a community around this book. Our community will write letters to the most influential members of our communities. We will start with the presidents, vice presidents, and CEOs of the country, the local communities, schools, businesses, religious organizations, political groups, civil rights groups, and so on. You are on the front line, responsible to write letters to everyone you believe can make a difference. Your letter will ask the receiver to write their own letter to whomever they feel they can influence. Your letter is up to you. Below is my letter to you .

Dear Reader,

You have a vital role in the collective experience of the human race. You can change the world one loving, compassionate, embracive statement at a time. I write to you to ask for your forgiveness and to offer my forgiveness to you as well. We need you now to honor your position as a leader and reach out to everyone you know to return the world to brotherhood, sisterhood, morality, integrity, and equal justice for all. Thank you.

Love,
Matthew

The Letter Writing Worksheet in the Think Again Workbook will enable you to determine who you want to write to, decide on your topics, and make a specific request.

"When your eyes have found the strength
To constantly speak to the world.
All that is most dear
To your own
Life,

When your hands, feet and tongue
Can perform in that are unison
That comforts this longing earth
With the knowledge

Your soul,
Your soul has been groomed
In His city of love;

And when you can make others laugh
With jokes
That belittle no one
And your words always unite,

Hafiz will vote for you to be
The minister of every country in
This universe.

Hafiz does vote for you my dear.
I vote for you
To be
God."

Hafiz

THINK AGAIN WORKBOOK

For your FREE Think Again Workbook

Visit: www.ThinkAgain.co

Unique IP Q&A Worksheet

Remembering and maintaining an unbreakable bond to Unique IP is critical to your spiritual health and growth. Answer the following questions to tap in and remember.

	Common Question	Unique IP Answer
Ex	When someone offends you, how do you react?	Since I have no control over how and what others say, I direct my words and responses through the voice of God, regardless of how or what I think I heard.
1	When someone offends you, how do you react?	
2	How do you justify resentments or grudges?	
3	What is the benefit of intentional thinking?	
4	Why is it important to be aware of the thoughts that develop from your feelings?	
5	What are the best ways to identify and remove ego thoughts from your Unique IP?	
6	Who is responsible for your happiness and why?	
7	What is the best way to create change?	
8	Why is change healthy?	
9	How do you define growth?	
10	How do you heal relationship tension?	

Fear, Doubt, and Worry Worksheet

Write down topics that trigger fear doubt and worry. Then write down results you have experienced from your fear doubt and worry.

When I feel fear, doubt, and worry about:	I receive
Ex. money	financial challenges
Ex. losing	loss
Ex. health	illness
1.	
2.	
3.	
4.	
5.	
6.	
7.	
8.	
9.	
10.	

Thought List Worksheet

If your thoughts were either good or bad (Unique IP or ego), and if you were aware, then it would be easy to change your bad thoughts to good thoughts if or when they showed up in your mind. Write down ego thoughts that you remember having and then write down the Unique IP thoughts that come from inside, the ones you know to be true.

	Ego Thought	Unique IP Thought
Ex	Strike your enemy before they strike you.	When others appear to be against you, see through the eyes of God and recognize the brother or sister standing before you.
1		
2		
3		
4		
5		
6		
7		
8		
9		
10		

Intention Statements Worksheet

Intention statements are calls to action, to yourself. State your intentional idea and write how this idea can change your life. When ideas turn to words and words turn to actions, you will see what you wrote about come to life.

	Intentional Idea	How this idea can change your life
Ex	I intend to focus on Unique IP to guide decision making in my life.	I will live, love, work, and play with thoughts and actions that make me and the people in my life feel incredible about our relationships.
1		
2		
3		
4		
5		
6		
7		
8		
9		
10		

The Future You Worksheet

Write about a current situation that describes a way you are acting or feeling that you are not satisfied with. Then write how you wish that situation could be, in your ideal world. Finally, write one action that you can take as a first step to realize your ideal future you.

	Current You	Future You	Today's Action
Ex	Emotionally unavailable to the people I love	Free to express myself, open to hear honest feedback, and able to be present	Sit down with my wife, express how much I appreciate her and our relationship, share with her one area of my life where I feel vulnerable, and ask for help
1			
2			
3			
4			
5			
6			
7			
8			
9			
10			

True or False Worksheet

This worksheet will enable you to list your beliefs about yourself, others, and the world around you. Your goal is to evaluate whether the statements that you make every day are true or false.

	Statement	True	False
Ex	I am not good enough to succeed at this task		X
Ex	There are 24 hours in the day	X	
1.			
2.			
3.			
4.			
5.			
6.			
7.			
8.			
9.			
10.			

Unique IP Worksheet

Write down the greatest qualities about yourself, the ones that have been with you from birth. These are the qualities that largely make up who you are, the ones that, when you are aligned, bring the greatest connection, joy, and love to your life. Then write your thoughts about your gifts and the benefits of thinking the way you do.

	My Unique IP	My Thoughts	Benefit(s) of my thinking
Ex	Compassionate	Another person's actions reflect what they are going through internally.	When I sense someone is out of sync, I ask simple questions to allow for further communication.
1			
2			
3			
4			
5			
6			
7			
8			
9			
10			

Think About Your Thoughts Worksheet

Write down prominent thoughts you have about yourself, family, friends, work, religion and life itself. Then, write your thoughts about your thoughts.

	Thought	Thoughts about your thoughts
Ex	I wish I had more money.	I should think about an action I can take today, working within my Unique IP, to begin the process of earning more money.
1		
2		
3		
4		
5		
6		
7		
8		
9		
10		

New Statement Technique Worksheet

Write a feeling that triggers a statement. Then, write the statement. If the statement is holding you back from moving forward, write a new statement. Replace the old statement with the new statement by remembering and stating every time the trigger shows up.

	Trigger	Old Statement	New Statement
Ex	Feeling Stagnant	I hate when my life is at a standstill.	Time to turn inward to Unique IP for clues on where and how to make a necessary change.
1			
2			
3			
4			
5			
6			
7			
8			
9			
10			

Worldview Challenge Worksheet

Choose the one answer that best describes how you feel about each statement listed below:

Worldview	Strongly Agree	Agree	Disagree	Strongly Disagree
1. Love is an important part of the solution to every challenge.				
2. Hate is justifiable if you have a good reason.				
3. Resentments will help you solve any problem.				
4. The best way to explain the world is to recognize a supernatural power greater and wiser than human beings.				
5. White entitlement is a social impediment.				
6. There is no place for racism in the world.				
7. Everyone is born good.				
8. If we want to experience the joys of life, we must be graciously willing to experience the hardships.				
9. God is omnipresent.				
10. God cannot be proven, therefore is not real.				

Worldview Challenge Worksheet

	A	B	C	D
11	Black and brown skin people	face racism regularly	are treated equally in today's society	get what they deserve	deserve a level playing field
12	Defending our country's borders is important	but assisting people in need from around the world is more important	to maintain good relationships with others	to keep America strong	to keep criminals out
13	In general, people with more money	are smarter and better than those with less	always abuse their power and privilege	usually oppress the rest of society	are often privileged, talented, focused, and lucky
14	When I experience hardship, I usually	feel sad and isolated	question God	ask, "Why me?"	appreciate the hardship and use my pain to help others in similar situations
15	When I think about God, I	believe God is made up by the guys who wrote the Bible	think that if God was our creator, there would not be so much hate	believe that God created the universe, is omnipresent, and fully able	remember that science is responsible for our existence

THINK AGAIN WORKBOOK

Select the pre-written response that best describes how you feel about each statement listed below:

	A	B	C	D
16	When I travel to other parts of the world, I	expect to have a lot in common with people	realize why there is so much conflict	clearly see how different we are	expand my view
17	The majority of black and brown men and women in prison	deserve to be there	have been wrongfully convicted	had odds stacked against them	require friendship and compassion
18	When someone says something to offend me	the best response is revenge	it is best to ignore them	I feel compassion and curiosity	I hold a grudge
19	I prefer to do things that	I already know how to do	allow me to avoid new difficult challenges	present new opportunities	keep me in my comfort zone
20	Gun violence in America is	statistically irrelevant	understandable	unacceptable	on the rise
21	When I have a challenge in my life, I	realize that God is not always on my side	identify the people involved and reprimand them	look at myself, find the lesson, and implement change	Go inward and do my best to solve the problem
22	When I give things away that are meaningful to me, I	lose a big part of myself	feel appreciation for my ability to bring joy to someone else	resent the person who is receiving my gift	expect something in return

		A	B	C	D
23	When I feel fear, doubt, and worry, I	call my closest friends to talk about it	sit and stew over what might happen	recognize my ego at work and shift gears	get really down
24	My words are important because	I need to tell people what to do	they reflect how I feel and think	they prove that I am educated	it's good to hear myself speak
25	Love is	everything	nothing	a fairytale	love
26	Children are	pure	jaded	annoying	powerful
27	Death is	scary	horrible	peaceful	a continuation
28	Hate is	normal	okay	ego	wrong
29	Compassion is	selfless	selfish	a waste of time	interesting
30	Appreciation is	useless	thankful	deserving	obligatory

The Giving Worksheet

Write down 10 things you receive from people in your life and from life itself. Include all things that are notable, whether good or bad. You will further list the things you know you give that contribute to what you are receiving.

What you receive	What you give to trigger what you receive
Ex. Even though I am honest, people often don't trust me.	I often confirm conversations in writing, which might indicate my lack of trust in others.
1.	
2.	
3.	
4.	
5.	
6.	
7.	
8.	
9.	
10.	

The Forgiveness Worksheet

Write down 10 grudges or resentments that you hold and the people (including yourself) that you forgive.

	My unjustified resentment is:	With all my heart, I forgive:
Ex.	My brother cheated me and treated me with a lack of love.	Fred
Ex.	When my father was angry at me, I allowed my ego to justify returning the anger.	Myself
1.		
2.		
3.		
4.		
5.		
6.		
7.		
8.		
9.		
10.		

Hierarchy of Thought Worksheet

The hierarchy of thought starts on the inside and then shows up on the outside. How do you see yourself thinking about these categories?

	Positive	Negative	Your Views
Karmic Thoughts	Equality Compassion Love	Superiority Phobic	
Worldviews	Brotherhood Sisterhood Appreciation	Racism Prejudice	
Feelings	Empowerment Love	Fearful Doubtful	
Thoughts	Togetherness Forgiveness	Hate Anger Resentment	
Words	Can Yes Love God	Cannot No Hate	
Actions	Unifying Giving Sensitive Inclusive	Oppressive Mistrusting Belittling	

Self-Identity Worksheet

When you describe yourself to the world, what do you say? Examine the words you use and evaluate whether they belong to your inner world or to your outer world.

Self-Identity Statement	Inner World	Outer World
Ex. I am a lawyer		X
Ex. I am an entrepreneur		X
Ex. I am a teacher to my children	X	
1.		
2.		
3.		
4.		
5.		
6.		
7.		
8.		
9.		
10.		

Letter Writing Worksheet

We will form a community around this book. Our community will write letters to the most influential members of our communities. Your letter will ask the receiver to write their own letter to whomever they feel they can influence. Your letter is up to you. Below is my letter to you.

> Dear Reader,
> You have a vital role in the collective experience of the human race. You can change the world one loving, compassionate, embracive statement at a time. I write to you to ask for your forgiveness and to offer my forgiveness to you as well. We need you now to honor your position as a leader and reach out to everyone you know to return the world to brotherhood, sisterhood, morality, integrity, and equal justice for all. Thank you.
>
> *Love,*
> *Matthew*

Who will you write to?	What is your topic?	What is your ask?
Ex. President of US	Words	Speak with compassion
Ex. Religious Leader	Acceptance	Accept and embrace everyone inclusively
1.		
2.		
3.		
4.		
5.		

Thoughts and Words Worksheet

Do the following thoughts turn into the following words? Feel free to add to the list of words to best reflect the what you say after thinking the thoughts listed.

	Thought	Words
1	Trust	Fair, open, balanced
2	Distrust	Unfair, closed, imbalanced
3	Good	Yes, appreciate, excited
4	Bad	No, not okay, wrong
5	Kind	Love, aligned, trusting, relationship
6	Unkind	Hate, dislike, mean
7	Succeed	Win, champion, best
8	Fail	Lose, no chance, worst
9	Hopeful	We can, we will, yes
10	Hopeless	Not possible, we can't, no

"Challenging the meaning of life is the truest expression of the state of being human."
— Viktor Frankl

About the Author

MATTHEW SCHWAM IS KNOWN BEST as a visionary for creating inspirational, iconic holiday displays in New York City and around the world. He has founded and built businesses providing endless hours of creativity, management, and mentorship to colleagues and customers over the past 20 years. The mission of his business is to deliver beauty to the world.

On his 40th birthday, he was clinically diagnosed with bipolar disorder. In the same way that Think Again encourages readers to identify challenges, tackle them with awareness and create solution-based change, he has largely learned to manage the false narrative of negativity that previously impacted his life for many years.

Fortunately, with great mentors, tools, unending desire to live each day to the fullest, he built a life of purpose and alignment that prepared him to deliver the lessons of *Think Again*.

He lives in Connecticut with his wife Jillian and their children. His personal mission is to deliver thoughtful simplified understanding to the complexities of one's life. His passions are art, creation, sports and spending loving time with friends and family.

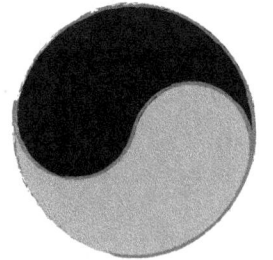

www.ingramcontent.com/pod-product-compliance
Lightning Source LLC
Chambersburg PA
CBHW071208070526
44584CB00019B/2965